FRANZ KAFKA: Pictures of a Life

Kafka in front of the Oppelt House, the apartment building where his family lived. Prague, the Altstädter Ring (Old Town Square), around the time that Kafka was working on *The Castle* (1922).

FRANZ KAFKA:
Pictures of a Life

KLAUS WAGENBACH

TRANSLATED FROM THE GERMAN
BY ARTHUR S. WENSINGER

PANTHEON BOOKS
NEW YORK

English translation Copyright © 1984 by Random House, Inc.
All rights reserved under International and Pan-American Copyright
Conventions. Published in the United States by Pantheon Books, a division
of Random House, Inc., New York, and simultaneously in Canada by
Random House of Canada Limited, Toronto.
Originally published in Germany as two separate books:
Franz Kafka: Bilder aus seinem Leben by Verlag Klaus Wagenbach.
Copyright © 1983 by Verlag Klaus Wagenbach.
Kafka by Rowohlt Taschenbuch Verlag GmbH. Copyright © 1964 by
Rowohlt Taschenbuch Verlag GmbH.

Library of Congress Cataloging in Publication Data
Wagenbach, Klaus.
   Franz Kafka: pictures of a life.
   1. Kafka, Franz, 1883–1924—Iconography.
2. Authors, Austrian—20th century—Iconography.
I. Title.
PT2621.A26Z97613 1984   833'.912   84-42666
ISBN 0-394-53666-5
ISBN 0-394-72573-5 (pbk.)

*Since the permissions acknowledgments cannot be accommodated
on this copyright page, they appear on page 221.*

Designed by Naomi Osnos

Manufactured in the United States of America
First American Edition

A NOTE ON THIS EDITION

In format this English-language edition of Klaus Wagenbach's *Franz Kafka: Bilder aus seinem Leben* is nearly identical
with the German original. The Foreword and the introductory texts to each section are direct translations of the original. There are, however, two substantive additions to the
German book, which we felt were called for. First, to
augment the brief biographical data in the introductory
texts, we have incorporated a number of quotations from
Kafka's letters, diaries, and notebooks; these were drawn
from the works cited in the Partial List of Sources. Second,
where it was felt that the reader would be helped by translations of the texts illustrated within the photographs
(documents, letters, newspaper articles, passages from
Kafka's works, and the like), we have provided these either
in the captions or, for longer texts, in the Appendix.

A.S.W.

Contents

Prague, center of the Old City, the Altstädter Ring (Old Town Square), around 1890. A view of the Nikolomarkt, or Saint Nicholas Market Fair, held annually at Christmas time and often mentioned by Kafka. On the left, the Kinsky Palais, where Kafka attended the Imperial and Royal Altstädter Gymnasium from 1893 to 1901 (on the top floor) and where his father's fancy-goods store was located after 1912 (on the ground floor to the right of the entrance).

In the background, the Týn Church. At center, the Column of the Virgin, a favorite meeting place of Kafka and his friend Max Brod.

At the far right, the beginning of the Zeltnergasse, which runs to the Powder Tower. The Kafkas lived on this street from 1897 to 1907; the father's business was also located here from the 1890s until 1912.

Foreword

I first began to assemble this collection of photographs of Kafka's life and times more than thirty years ago. My initial impulse came from the dissatisfaction I felt with the surfeit of Kafka interpretations whose speculative nature increased in direct proportion to their authors' ignorance of the historical, personal, and linguistic circumstances in which Kafka's work came into being. Until the mid-1950s, at least, Kafka was a writer who seemed to have come from some no man's land. This was especially true in France and England, the very countries initially responsible for fostering Kafka's international reputation.

The impression of Kafka's writing as homeless and deracinated is, to be sure, also due in part to its high degree of abstraction, its paucity of realistic detail, its few topographical points of reference and infrequent time indications; the absence of a narrator to take the reader by the hand; and the parabolic and dialectic narrative structure, which not only permits an endless number of interpretative possibilities but even insists on them. In sum, all the characteristics that have established Kafka as a father of modern literature: alienation, abstraction, and dialectic.

There are two possible ways of reading this book: either as a purely visual capturing of the details of the life of an important writer from Prague between the years 1883 and 1924, or as a pictorial demonstration of the gap between factual background and literary formulation.

Both approaches are possible, and both seem reasonable to me. There is one proviso, however: the preservation of historical perspective. All previously published volumes of photographic material on Kafka, with their intention of showing "how Kafka would see Prague today if he were still alive," are unsatisfactory precisely because of their failure to maintain this historical distance. What we get from them are mostly atmospheric shots of cobblestone streets taken against the light, or of the Emperor Charles Bridge at dusk.

The task I set myself was to link the images of particular places to a particular time in history, to present photographs of buildings taken at the very time Kafka lived in them, pictures of people at the age they were when Kafka met them, and pictures of places from the years in which Kafka visited them. This entailed a considerable expenditure of time and patience, substantial research in archives, and trips to all the places Kafka knew. Finally, it also meant expanding the usual literary and historical viewpoint to include the so-called everyday world. What did the Nikolomarkt (*opposite*), which Kafka described in his works, actually look like? What about his bicycle, his motorcycle? How exactly are we to picture a typical office of the period? Or the Pomological Institute, where Kafka wanted to learn gardening? Or the Civilschwimmschule, the swimming and boating school where Kafka kept his rowboat? And what did those boats look like, the ones he called "drowners of poor souls"? Or the factories he had to inspect as an official of the Workers Accident Insurance Company?

The principle of historical fidelity to the contemporaneous image could not, to be sure, be everywhere satisfied. It was astonishing enough to discover that the old "water-cure sanitorium," Dr. Schweinburg's spa in Zuckmantel, the scene of Kafka's first love affair, still existed (albeit in quite another guise), as well as the house of Kafka's uncle Siegfried Löwy, the famous country doctor in Triesch. Here and in a handful of other instances, present-day photographs had to suffice. I hope they will be forgiven, just as I hope that readers will indulge my penchant for including the occasional picture that might seem a bit far-fetched. I would ask them to sympathize, for example, with my temptation to search for and, once they were finally located, to include some stereopticon slides from the "Kaiser-panorama," an amusement arcade described in Kafka's journal of his trip to Friedland—a lucky find, which I hope will delight the perusers of these pictures as it did me.

In order to include these many discoveries, I have kept the text to a reasonable minimum. Whoever may wish to learn more is referred to the many general studies of Kafka that have appeared in recent years.

For the rest, the pictures that follow are intended "to impart knowledge," as Red Peter (the ape in "Report to an Academy") says, and also to give pleasure; for, as he goes on, "everyone on earth feels a tickling at the heels."

A Brief Chronology of Kafka's Life

1883

Franz Kafka born on July 3 in Prague-Altstadt, the first child of the merchant Hermann Kafka (1852–1931) and his wife, Julie, née Löwy (1856–1934). His brothers and sisters: Georg (born 1885, died fifteen months later); Heinrich (born 1887, died six months later); Gabriele, called Elli (1889–1941); Valerie, called Valli (1890–1942); and Ottilie, called Ottla (1892–1943).

1889–1893

Attends the Deutsche Knabenschule (German Primary School for Boys) on the Fleischmarkt in Prague.

1893–1901

Attends the humanistic Staatsgymnasium mit deutscher Unterrichssprache in Prag-Altstadt, a high school where all instruction was in German. Emil Gschwind was head master for Kafka's class. First writings (destroyed).

1897

Friendship with Rudolf Illowý; discussions of social issues and problems.

1898

Friendship with Hugo Bergmann, Ewald Felix Přibram, and particularly Oskar Pollak (until 1904). Regular reader of the cultural journal *Der Kunstwart (Guardian of the Arts),* edited by Ferdinand Avenarius. Under the influence of his natural history instructor, Adolf Gottwald, reads Darwin and Haeckel.

1900

Summer vacation with Uncle Siegfried, the country doctor in Triesch, and at Roztok, the parents' vacation resort. Reads Nietzsche.

1901

Graduates from *Gymnasium.* First vacation by himself, on the German North Sea islands of Norderney and Helgoland. In autumn, begins studies at the German University of Prague: chemistry for the first two weeks, then law; also hears lectures in art history.

1902

Pursues German studies during summer semester. Summer vacation in Liboch and in Triesch. Trip to Munich with plans to continue German studies there. Returns for winter semester to Prague University, where he continues with law. First meeting with Max Brod.

1903

In summer, state examinations in history of law, followed by stay at Dr. Lahmann's Sanatorium in Weisser Hirsch near Dresden. Afterward travels to Southern Bohemia.

1904

Begins work on "Description of a Struggle" ("Beschreibung eines Kampfes").

1905

Spends summer at the Schweinburg Sanatorium in Zuckmantel. First love affair. Visits aunts Anna and Julie in Strakonitz with his mother and three sisters. In the following winter, beginning of regular meetings with friends Oskar Baum, Felix Weltsch, and Max Brod.

1906

Apprenticeship in law office. July 18, graduates with degree in law. Again vacations in Zuckmantel. In autumn, begins one-year legal internship, first in the *Landgericht* (provincial high court), then in the *Strafgericht* (criminal court). Writes "Wedding Preparations in the Country" ("Hochzeitsvorbereitungen auf dem Lande").

1907

Spends summer in Triesch. Meets Hedwig Weiler. In October assumes temporary post with the Assicurazioni Generali, a private insurance firm in Prague.

1908

First publication: eight prose pieces in the literary magazine *Hyperion,* edited by Franz Blei, later reprinted as part of volume of pieces *Meditation (Betrachtung).* In

July, position as a junior assistant with the Arbeiter-Unfall-Versicherungs-Anstalt für das Königreich Böhmen in Prag (The Workers Accident Insurance Company for the Kingdom of Bohemia in Prague), a job "with standard hours." First trip for the company, to Tetschen. One-week vacation in Spitzberg in the Bohemian Forest. Beginning of close friendship with Max Brod. Numerous short trips to the countryside around Prague. Spends time in cabarets, coffeehouses, *cafés chantants*.

1909
Vacation with Max and Otto Brod in Riva on Lake Garda. Writes "The Aeroplanes in Brescia" ("Die Aeroplane in Brescia"). Numerous business trips: Tetschen, Pilsen, Maffersdorf. Begins keeping diaries.

1910
In May, promoted to *Concipist* (a junior official) for his firm. Visits electioneering assemblies and Socialist mass meetings. Sees Yiddish acting troupe. Attends evening lectures at Berta Fanta's intellectual salon. Vacation trip to Paris with Max and Otto Brod. Business trip to Gablonz. In December, a week in Berlin.

1911
Many business trips to Reichenberg and Friedland in Northern Bohemia, and to Warnsdorf, where he meets the natural-health practitioner Schnitzer. Vacation trip with Max Brod to the north Italian lakes and Paris, followed by a week alone at the Fellenberg natural-health sanatorium in Erlenbach near Zurich. Financed by his father, he becomes a silent partner in the asbestos factory of his brother-in-law Josef Pollak. Friendship with the Yiddish actor Yitzak Löwy. Pursues interest in Judaism.

1912
First draft of *Amerika* (Brod's title for *Der Verschollene*, "the man who was never heard from again"). Summer vacation trip with Max Brod to Weimar, followed by three weeks alone at another natural-health resort, Justs Jungborn (Just's Fountain of Youth) in the Harz Mountains. In August, puts together his first book, *Meditation,* and first meets Felice Bauer. In September, "The Judgment" ("Das Urteil"). In October, considers

suicide when his family insists that he take over directorship of the "hated" asbestos factory. November–December, "The Metamorphosis" ("Die Verwandlung"). Business trips to Kratzau and Leitmeritz. Second draft of *Amerika.* Publication of *Meditation.*

1913
Business trips to Leitmeritz and Aussig. Promotion to vice-secretary. Visits Felice Bauer in Berlin three times. Gardening work at the Pomological Institute in Troja near Prague. In September, trip with Director Marschner to the "International Congress for Rescue Services and Accident Prevention" in Vienna; continues trip alone via Trieste, Venice, Verona, and Desenzano to Riva and the sanatorium of Dr. von Hartungen. Love affair with "the Swiss girl." Publication of *The Stoker (Der Heizer,* later to be the first chapter of *Amerika).* Meets Grete Bloch.

1914
Visits Felice twice in Berlin. She comes to Prague. Their official engagement in Berlin, June 1. Trip to Hellerau. On July 12, the "courtroom drama at the hotel" in Berlin; the engagement is broken. Trip with Ernst Weiss to the Danish Baltic Sea resort of Marielyst. Beginning in August, lives first with sister Valli on the Bilekgasse, then with Elli on the Nerudagasse. Works on *The Trial (Der Prozess).* Writes "In the Penal Colony" ("In der Strafkolonie").

1915
First reunion with Felice. In March, moves into his own quarters, a single room on the Langengasse. Trip to Hungary in April with Elli. In July, visit to Frankenstein Sanatorium near Rumburg. The writer Carl Sternheim presents the Fontane Prize money to Kafka. *The Metamorphosis* published.

1916
July: ten days with Felice Bauer at Marienbad. Publication of collection of stories *The Judgment.* Gives public reading of "In the Penal Colony" in Munich. Beginning in November, in a small house on the Alchimistengasse rented by sister Ottla, writes the stories later collected in *A Country Doctor (Ein Landarzt).*

1917

In March, takes an apartment in the Schönborn Palais. Studies Hebrew. Travels with Felice to visit her sister in Budapest. Second engagement to Felice. In August, a hemorrhage, onset of tuberculosis of the lungs. In September, moves to Ottla's country house in Zürau, where she is studying agricultural methods. In December, second engagement broken.

1918

In May, takes up insurance company work again. Renews interest in gardening in Troja. In September, garden work and recuperation in Turnau. Returns to Prague. December spent in Schelesen.

1919

Schelesen. Meets Julie Wohryzek. Back in Prague by April. Engagement to Julie Wohryzek. Publication of collection of stories *In the Penal Colony*. Returns to Schelesen in November; writes *Letter to His Father (Brief an den Vater);* meets Minze Eisner. In December, back to Prague.

1920

Promotion to company secretary. Writes aphorisms for the collection *He (Er)*. Acquaintance with Gustav Janouch. In April, to Merano. Correspondence with Milena Jesenská. Vienna. Summer and autumn in Prague, where he writes many short stories. Breaks engagement to Julie Wohryzek. Publication of *A Country Doctor.* In December, enters the sanatorium at Matliary in the High Tatra.

1921

Matliary. Friendship with Robert Klopstock. Returns to Prague in the autumn. In October, places all his diaries in Milena's hands.

1922

January–February in Spindelmühle, Silesia. Begins writing *The Castle (Das Schloss)*. Promotion to first secretary. Works on stories for *A Hunger Artist (Ein Hungerkünstler)*. Retires in June on medical grounds. From end of June to mid-September, with Ottla and her family in Planá on the Luschnitz at their summer home.

1923

Takes up Hebrew studies again; considers emigration to Palestine. Spends July in Müritz on the Baltic coast. Meets Dora Diamant. August and September, with Ottla in Schelesen. At end of September, moves to Berlin to live with Dora Diamant. Writes "A Little Woman" ("Eine kleine Frau") and "The Burrow" ("Der Bau").

1924

Back in Prague by March. Writes "Josephine the Singer" ("Josefine die Sängerin"). In the company of Dora Diamant and Robert Klopstock, Kafka enters the Hoffmann Sanatorium in Kierling bei Klosterneuburg, on the outskirts of Vienna, where he dies on June 3, in his forty-first year. Burial in Prague. Final collection of stories, *A Hunger Artist,* is published that summer.

Family and Childhood

It was not until they were adults that either of Kafka's parents came to Prague. The physical distance they had to travel to get there was not particularly great in either case; but their paths from the provinces of Bohemia to the capital city originated not only at two quite different points of the compass but also in two altogether opposite social milieus.

Kafka's mother, Julie Löwy, came from the town of Podiebrad on the Elbe, about thirty miles to the east of Prague. She was the daughter of a respected and well-to-do German-Jewish family of textile merchants and brewery owners. Kafka's father, Hermann Kafka, came from a tiny Bohemian village called Wossek, in the district of Pisek, about sixty miles south of Prague, where he grew up in poverty-stricken circumstances. His father was a butcher and performed the kosher slaughtering for the village. The family spoke both Czech and German.

The maternal forebears of Kafka's mother (the Porias family, who had lived in Podiebrad for generations) included a number of pious Talmudists, scholars, physicians, converts, bachelors, and solitary eccentrics, frequently considered by local society to be a bit "touched."

In Hebrew my name is Amschel, like my mother's maternal grandfather, whom my mother, who was six years old when he died, can remember as a very pious and learned man with a long, white beard. She remembers how she had to take hold of the toes of the corpse and ask forgiveness for any offense she may have committed against her grandfather. She also remembers her grandfather's many books which lined the walls. He

bathed in the river every day, even in winter, when he chopped a hole in the ice for his bath. My mother's mother died of typhus at an early age. From the time of this death her grandmother became melancholy, refused to eat, spoke with no one; once, a year after the death of her daughter, she went for a walk and did not return, her body was found in the Elbe. An even more learned man than her grandfather was my mother's great-grandfather, Christians and Jews held him in equal honor; during a fire a miracle took place as a result of his piety, the flames jumped over and spared his house while the houses around it burned down. He had four sons, one was converted to Christianity and became a doctor. All but my mother's grandfather died young. He had one son, whom my mother knew as crazy Uncle Nathan, and one daughter, my mother's mother.

On the mother's paternal side (the Löwys from Humpoletz, a small town in eastern Bohemia), practical businessmen predominated, mostly textile and fabric merchants who, more often than not, were inclined to assimilate. Julie's father, Jakob Löwy, by family background also a dry-goods merchant, bought the Podiebrad brewery. He married twice. There were four offspring from his first marriage, to Esther Porias: Kafka's mother, Julie, and her three brothers, Alfred, Richard, and Josef. After Esther's early death at twenty-nine, Jakob Löwy married Julie Heller from Postelberg, a distant relative of the Porias family. With her he had two more sons, Rudolf and Siegfried. The family moved to Prague about 1880.

Kafka enjoyed a good relationship with most of his five maternal uncles, especially with Siegfried, the country doctor in Triesch whom Kafka often visited, and with Alfred, the director of a Spanish railroad company who made frequent visits from Madrid to Prague.

Kafka's mother had lost her own mother and grandparents when she was still very young and grew up under the sole guidance of her father and stepmother from the time she was four. As the only daughter she had to assume family responsibilities at an early age and take care of her five younger brothers. Consequently, she developed early that blend of modesty and energy that Kafka later characterized as a special legacy of the Löwys: "defiance, sensitivity, a sense of justice, restlessness."

The parents of Kafka's father, like their ancestors, both came from Wossek, indeed, from the same little lane in the lower village, which in the year 1850 had about a hundred inhabitants, all of them Jews, with their own cemetery, their own German-speaking school, and their own synagogue. The Czech-speaking Christian peasants and farmers lived in the upper village. Rising above the whole town was a castle on an extensive estate (with a top-heavy administration). The entire surrounding countryside belonged to the castle's owner, the newly ennobled Eduard von Doubek. (Numerous details of this constellation had a direct effect on the conception of Kafka's novel *The Castle*.)

Jakob Kafka, the butcher, was generally respected and feared in the community by virtue of his great strength and size. His wife Franziska (Fanny), née Platowski, is described as considerate, kind, and much admired for her knowledge of folk medicine. The family's house, number 30, is one of the squat cottages common in Bohemia, originally with a thatched roof and a single ground-floor room in which the six children grew up: two daughters, Anna and Julie, and four sons, Filip, Heinrich, Ludwig, and Hermann, Kafka's father.

With the relaxation of many of the laws directed against the Jews and the awakening of Czech nationalism in the latter half of the nineteenth century, the exodus of the Jews from the provinces to the large cities began. Indeed, in 1889 Kafka's grandfather was the last Jew to be buried in the Wossek cemetery. By that time his sons and daughters were already settled as merchants in larger towns and cities—in nearby Strakonitz, and in Prague, Kolin, and Leitmeritz.

Among his father's relatives, Kafka was closest in later years to his Uncle Ludwig (a merchant and later an insurance agent in Prague; his daughter Irma worked in Hermann Kafka's store and was a close friend of Franz's sister Ottla) and to his "merry" Uncle Filip, a merchant in Kolin. Both Filip's wife, Klara, and several of their children who eventually emigrated to America became models for certain characters in the novel *Amerika*. Kafka catalogues his paternal legacy as "strength, robust health, articulateness, self-satisfaction, endurance," an outspoken "will for living, for business, and for conquest."

In 1882 Kafka's father, at the age of thirty, married and set himself up in a *Galanteriewarenhandlung*, a fancy-goods store dealing in walking sticks, parasols, haberdashery, and other fashionable articles. Prior to that he had been an itinerant tradesman for a number of years, living at the edge of the former ghetto (which was to be torn down twenty years later), while the woman he was to marry was living with her family in the elegant Smetana House on the Altstädter Ring (Old Town Square), scarcely a hundred yards away.

A year after their marriage, on the third of July, 1883, Franz Kafka was born in the "House of the Tower" where the Enge Gasse and the Karpfengasse intersect—again, just at the edge of the ghetto. In the early years of the marriage the family moved with uncommon frequency. By the time Kafka was of school age in 1889, they had changed their residence five times, proof of the father's mercantile ambition, that "will for business" of which Kafka wrote, his striving for financial success and social acceptance. Everything else was secondary, including his family life and the children's upbringing. Decades later, Kafka wrote to his fiancée: "I am the eldest of six brothers and sisters; two brothers somewhat younger than myself died as little children through the fault of the doctors. Then things were quiet for a time. I was the only child. . . . I lived that way a long while, all by myself, and had to cope as best I could with nurses, old nannies, cantankerous cooks, and gloomy governesses, for my parents were forever occupied in the store." It was not until 1889, when Kafka was six, that his first sister, Elli, was born; a year later, Valli; and two years after that, Ottla, "the one I love most by far."

Kafka's upbringing was in perfect conformity with the code of the time. Yet despite the fact that his parents never allowed him to go without anything material, neither high buttoned shoes nor French governesses, neither toys to play with nor nursemaids nor piano lessons, Kafka as a child remained "unguided," full of "anxiety and dead-eyed seriousness."

Years later, in *Letter to His Father* (*Brief an den Vater*), he was to recall his state:

For me as a child everything you called out at me was positively a heavenly commandment, I never forgot it, it remained for me the most important means of forming a judgment of the world, above all of forming a judgment of you yourself, and there you failed entirely. Since as a child I was with you chiefly during meals, your teaching was to a large extent the teaching of proper behavior at table. What was brought to the table had to be eaten, the quality of food was not to be discussed—but you yourself often found the food inedible, called it "this swill," said "that beast" (the cook) had ruined it. . . .

. . . You, so tremendously the authoritative man, did not keep the commandments you imposed on me. Hence the world was for me divided into three parts: one in which I, the slave, lived under laws that had been invented only for me and which I could, I did not know why, never completely comply with; then a second world, which was infinitely remote from mine, in which you lived, concerned with government, with the issuing of orders and with the annoyance about their not being obeyed; and finally a third world where everybody else lived happily and free from orders and from having to obey. I was continually in disgrace. . . .

The firstborn son was in any event to have it better than his father (who nevertheless was not above using recollections of his own youthful suffering as one of his "principal methods of education"). For that reason, enrollment at the Deutsche Knabenschule (German Primary School for Boys) was stipulated for his son, even though at that very time Hermann Kafka was one of the founders of the first Prague synagogue in which the sermons were delivered in Czech. Always the circumspect businessman, he kept his mind simultaneously on his customers and on his son's future prospects. If his son were ever to succeed as a Jewish citizen in the Austro-Hungarian Empire, he would have to master the official language of the monarchy.

Nevertheless, Kafka spoke and wrote an almost flawless Czech throughout his life. And the path that paternal concern was determined to keep smooth for him was from the beginning quite rough, though instructive. Directly across from the Deutsche Knabenschule on the Fleischmarkt was the Czech grammar school; the inscription emblazoned over its entrance read "A Czech Child Belongs in the Czech School." Energetic disagreements between the pupils of the two "nationalities" were frequent (during one of the brawls Kafka's later friend Oskar Baum was blinded) and were, so to speak, a normal part of the daily pedagogical experience.

Every human being is peculiarly, and by virtue of his peculiarity, called to play his part in the world, but he must have a taste for his own peculiarity. So far as my experience went, both in school and at home the aim was to erase all trace of peculiarity. In this way they made the work of education easier, but also made life easier for the child, although, it is true, he first had to go through the pain caused him by discipline. A boy, for instance, who is in the middle of reading an exciting story in the evening will never be made to realize, merely by an argument bearing solely upon himself, that he must stop reading and go to bed. When in such a case I was told such things as that it was getting late, I was damaging my eyesight, I would be sleepy in the morning and find it hard to get up, and that the rubbishy, silly story wasn't worth it, although I could not specifically refute this, it was actually only because it all did not even come anywhere near beginning to be worth thinking about. . . . That was my peculiarity. It was suppressed by means of turning off the gas and leaving me without a light. By way of explanation they said: Everyone is going to bed, so you must go to bed too. I saw this and could not but believe it, although it made no sense to me. Nobody wants to carry out so many reforms as children do. Apart from this, in a certain respect, praiseworthy oppression, still, here, as almost everywhere, there remained a sting that no amount of reference to generality could make even a little blunter. . . .

. . . At that time, however, all I felt was the injustice done to me, I went to bed sadly, and here were the beginnings of that hatred which has in a certain respect determined my life in relation to my family and hence my life as a whole. . . . My peculiarity was not accorded any recognition; . . . there is no doubt that I did not profit from my peculiarities with that true gain which finally manifests itself as permanent self-confidence.

FAMILY
AND
CHILDHOOD

Hermann Kafka

Hermann Kafka (1852–1931), Kafka's father. Son of the butcher Jakob Kafka and his wife, Franziska (née Platowski), he was born and raised in Wossek, southern Bohemia. From 1882 on, he was a fancy-goods merchant in Prague.

Julie Löwy (1856–1934), Kafka's mother. Daughter of the textile merchant and brewer Jakob Löwy and his wife, Esther (née Porias), she was born and raised in Podiebrad on the Elbe. She married Hermann Kafka in 1882.

Podiebrad on the Elbe, marketplace, around 1880. The town, located east of Prague, is the birthplace of Kafka's mother. Her father, Jakob Löwy, owned the brewery on the bank of the river (upper left, with tower). The brewery stood at the edge of the ghetto (center background), which was no longer walled in by the time this picture was taken.

Opposite. Two photographs, taken somewhat later, when Podiebrad had become a resort town.
Top. The castle, seen from the Elbe.
Bottom. The spa. Kafka's parents visited here in later years.

Above. The house where Kafka's mother was born, brewery tower in the background (1956).

Right. The ruins of the brewery tower today.

Below. Kafka's mother's engagement photo (1882).

Jakob Löwy (1824–1910), Kafka's maternal grandfather, a textile merchant and brewer in Podiebrad.

Prague, Karlsgasse 24. Jakob Löwy spent his last years in this balcony apartment.

Below. Prague, the Altstädter Ring, with the Column of the Virgin and the Rathaus (City Hall), around 1900. Before her marriage, Kafka's mother lived in the Smetana House, the third building from the left.

19

The village of Wossek in the southern Bohemian district of Pisek, birthplace of Kafka's father.

Above left.　The lower village. Ruins of the synagogue (left) and the inn at the bridge (right).
Above right.　The castle of Sir Eduard von Doubek, in the upper village.
Below left.　The former inn in the upper village.
Below right.　The Jewish cemetery. In the far left background, the grave of Kafka's grandfather Jakob.

Above. Jakob Kafka's two-sided whetstone with the Hebrew inscription "Kosher."

Right. Kafka's paternal grandparents, Jakob Kafka (1814–1899), a butcher in Wossek, and his wife, Franziska (1816–1880/90).

Below. Lane known as "In the Jews' Quarter" in the lower village of Wossek. Kafka's father and his five brothers and sisters grew up in house number 30 (marked with an X). "We all had to sleep in the same room. . . . Even as a little boy I had to walk to work in Pisek."

Above. On the road between Wossek and Pisek.

Below. Old photograph of Pisek as seen from the banks of the Otava.

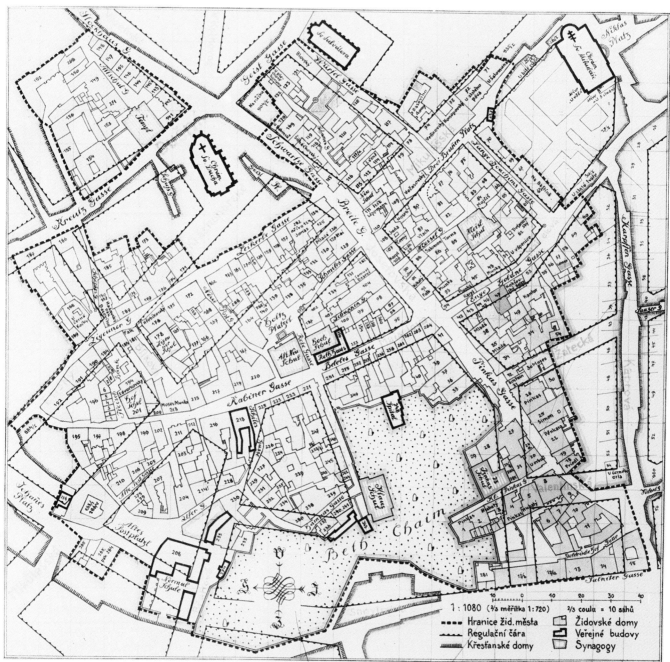

Plan of the Prague ghetto before its "sanitizing" (drawn around 1895). Located between the Old Town (Prague I) and the Moldau River, the ghetto was commonly known as the Josefstadt (Prague V) at the time Kafka was born. It was "a ramshackle quarter with junk shops, dives, and bordellos." With the urban renewal (euphemistically known as "sanitizing") at the turn of the century, new streets were cut through the ghetto and nearly all the old buildings were replaced with luxurious structures in the style of the Wilhelminian Era, the period of great economic growth and social change that began in 1871. The thick dotted line shows the boundaries of the old ghetto. The thinner lines strung with smaller dots indicate the outlines of the newly planned apartment complexes and streets. In the upper right corner are houses numbers 27/I and 30/I.

23

Above. On the right is the "House of the Golden Face" (number 30/I), photographed in 1895. Kafka's father lived here before his marriage in 1882. The larger building at the left marked the beginning of the ghetto, which at that time still existed as an architectural unit. Adjoining this complex at the right was the house (not shown) where Kafka was born. Both houses were demolished in 1897–1898.

Opposite above. Kafka's parents, photographed during the early years of their marriage.
Opposite below. House number 27/I at the corner of Karpfengasse and Enge Gasse (later Maiselgasse), where Kafka was born on July 3, 1883. In the far left background is the front of the "House of the Golden Face," still standing when this picture was taken.

Kafka's Family Tree

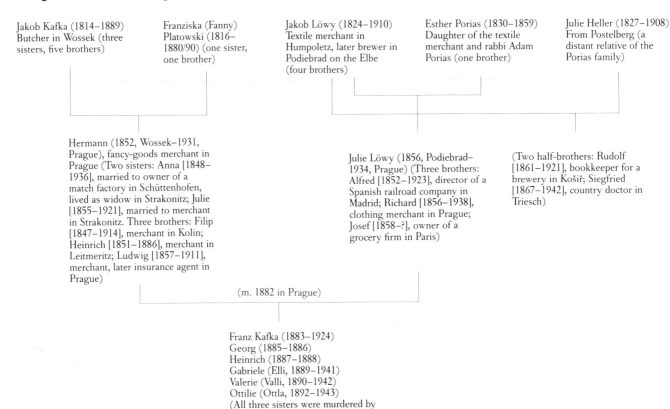

Jakob Kafka (1814–1889) Butcher in Wossek (three sisters, five brothers)

Franziska (Fanny) Platowski (1816–1880/90) (one sister, one brother)

Jakob Löwy (1824–1910) Textile merchant in Humpoletz, later brewer in Podiebrad on the Elbe (four brothers)

Esther Porias (1830–1859) Daughter of the textile merchant and rabbi Adam Porias (one brother)

Julie Heller (1827–1908) From Postelberg (a distant relative of the Porias family)

Hermann (1852, Wossek–1931, Prague), fancy-goods merchant in Prague (Two sisters: Anna [1848–1936], married to owner of a match factory in Schüttenhofen, lived as widow in Strakonitz; Julie [1855–1921], married to merchant in Strakonitz. Three brothers: Filip [1847–1914], merchant in Kolin; Heinrich [1851–1886], merchant in Leitmeritz; Ludwig [1857–1911], merchant, later insurance agent in Prague)

Julie Löwy (1856, Podiebrad–1934, Prague) (Three brothers: Alfred [1852–1923], director of a Spanish railroad company in Madrid; Richard [1856–1938], clothing merchant in Prague; Josef [1858–?], owner of a grocery firm in Paris)

(Two half-brothers: Rudolf [1861–1921], bookkeeper for a brewery in Košiř; Siegfried [1867–1942], country doctor in Triesch)

(m. 1882 in Prague)

Franz Kafka (1883–1924) Georg (1885–1886) Heinrich (1887–1888) Gabriele (Elli, 1889–1941) Valerie (Valli, 1890–1942) Ottilie (Ottla, 1892–1943) (All three sisters were murdered by the Nazis at Lodz and Auschwitz.)

Below. Kafka's birth certificate.

The two earliest photographs of Kafka.

Left. About one year old (1884).

Right. Probably taken in his second year. Almost thirty years later Kafka sent this picture to his fiancée, Felice Bauer, with the comment: "I enclose a picture of myself when I was perhaps five years old. At that time, that angry face was just for fun, but now I think of it as the secret truth. . . . I probably wasn't really five in this photograph—more like two—but you, as someone who likes children, would be a better judge of that than I. When there are children around I prefer to keep my eyes shut."

Kafka, approximately five years old.

"I was so insecure about everything that all I was really sure of was what I already held in my hands or my mouth or what was well on its way there."

PRAGUE *M. Klempfner* TEPLICE

28

Kafka's sisters.

Above. Ottla (born 1892), Elli (born 1889), and Valli (born 1890), around 1900. *Directly beneath.* Valli, Elli, Ottla, around 1898.

Below. The Altstädter Ring with the Kinsky Palais at the right. The third building from the left housed the father's first fancy-goods store in Prague, a simple street-front shop.

Above. View from the "little" to the "big" Altstädter Ring. In the background, the Týn Church. At the left, the tower of the City Hall (1838–1848) with the Clock of the Apostles (1490). In the left foreground, part of the Minuta House, where the Kafkas lived from 1889 to 1896 and where all three sisters were born. This 1896 painting shows Kafka's customary route to his first school, across the Ring, through the Little Týngasse, to the *Volksschule* (grammar school) on the Fleischmarkt, the meat-market square.

Far left. Kafka's mother at about the age of forty. *Near left.* Kafka, about four years old.

Below. View of the southeast corner of the "big" Altstädter Ring looking into the Zeltnergasse. The Kafkas had an apartment in the Sixt House (marked with an X) at Zeltnergasse 2 from 1888 to 1889. In the second house from the right, "The Unicorn Apothecary," Berta Fanta in later years held her literary salon, frequented by Gerhard Kowalewski, Rudolf Steiner, and Albert Einstein; Kafka also attended regularly.

Right. View into the Little Týngasse, through which Kafka walked daily on his way to grammar school accompanied by "the small, dry, withered, sharp-nosed cook." She and the housemaid were the two "respectable domestics" who looked after the little boy, since Kafka's mother was obliged to help her husband in the store and only returned home late in the evening.

Below. Kafka's grammar school from 1889 to 1893, the German Primary School for Boys on the Fleischmarkt. In Kafka's day the school had only a tiny yard, which meant that the pupils had to spend their recess either in the classrooms or in the corridors, which were decorated with such maxims as "Speech is silver. Silence is golden."

Kafka at about ten with
his sisters Valli (left) and
Elli (center).

Gymnasium and University

After Kafka's four years at primary school his father again had to make a choice between two modes of further education for his son: the *Realschule* ("modern high school") or the humanistic *Gymnasium*. His choice of the latter indicates either that the father had soon realized that despite his best efforts his son could not easily be molded into a proper businessman, or that he had made a conscious decision not even to make the attempt.

Whatever the motivation may have been—the father's insight, a partial disdain for his own way of life, or possibly social ambition on his son's behalf—when Kafka was ten years old it was determined to make "something better" out of him. The "correct" choice was the *Gymnasium*. The monarchy drew on these schools to fill its insatiable need for legal minds and civil servants. Yet even so, the expectation of success in these professions was severely limited, as is indicated by the following statistics for the Kingdom of Bohemia at the time Kafka attended the *Gymnasium*: in 1897, there were 1,048,000 pupils in the 5,500 primary schools but only 15,030 high school students in the 56 *Gymnasien* and *Realschulen;* and this already vastly diminished number must further be set against a mere 4,150 students at the two national universities, the Czech and the German, both in Prague. That is to say, of every 200 beginning pupils only one made it to university; and of these, only one in three was German-speaking. In the year Kafka earned his law degree, 1,480 students were enrolled at the German University.

The Imperial and Royal State Gymnasium with Instruction in the German Language, Prague-Altstadt, in the Kinsky Palais, where Kafka studied from 1893 to 1901, was considered the strictest of the seven such institutions in the city. Instruction in modern languages and literature was not offered (Kafka learned his French and later some English and Italian outside school); music, fine arts, and physical education were also elective pursuits. Beginning in the third year, nearly half the time was devoted to the two classical languages. The head master of Kafka's class for the entire period he was at the *Gymnasium* was the priest Emil Gschwind, an instructor in Latin and Greek and a superb, if strict, teacher. The most enduring impression, however, was made on Kafka by the natural history master, Adolf Gottwald, a convinced Darwinian with great pedagogical gifts.

Never shall I pass the first grade in grammar school, I thought, but I succeeded, I even got a prize; but I shall certainly not pass the entrance exam for the Gymnasium, but I succeeded; but now I shall certainly fail in the first year at the Gymnasium; no, I did not fail, and I went on and on succeeding. This did not produce any confidence, however; on the contrary, I was always convinced—and I positively had the proof of it in your forbidding expression—that the more I achieved, the worse the final outcome would inevitably be. Often in my mind's eye I saw the terrible assembly of the teachers (the Gymnasium is only the most integral example, but it was the same all around me), as they would meet, when I had passed the first class, and then in the second class, when I had passed that, and in the third, and so on, meeting in order to examine this unique, outrageous case, to discover how I, the most incapable and, in any case, the most ignorant of all, had succeeded in creeping up so far as this class, which now, when everybody's attention had at last been focused on me, would of course instantly spew me out, to the jubilation of all the righteous liberated from this nightmare.

Kafka's over-all evaluation for each of his first three years was "excellent"; after that, his performance was "average," except for mathematics, in which his grades were consistently miserable. He impressed his schoolmates as modest, unobtrusive, and reserved, as someone "always somehow surrounded by a glass wall." He made friends with very few of them, the notable exceptions being Rudolf Illowý, who was the first to introduce him to socialist thought (he withdrew from the school in 1898); Hugo Bergmann, a convinced Zionist even as an adolescent; Ewald Felix Přibram, who left the Church while still a pupil in the *Gymnasium* and whose father was the director of the insurance firm where Kafka was later to be employed; and finally, Oskar Pollak, the most mature member of the class and the one with whom Kafka joined the anticlerical club "Free School." Pollak remained Kafka's philosophic and artistic mentor well into their years together at the university. "For me, you were," he wrote to Pollak in 1903, "something like a window through which I could see the streets. I could not do that by myself, for tall though I am I do not yet reach to the windowsill."

Kafka's religious instruction, on the other hand, remained a rather feeble affair. His bar mitzvah in his thirteenth year at the Zigeuner (Gypsy) Synagogue entailed, as far as he was concerned, little more than "having laboriously to memorize a bit of prayer and recite it at the altar, then a short speech at home, which was likewise drummed into my head." And as far as his father was concerned, the event was more of a social than a religious rite; accordingly, he announced it, following the assimilationist custom, as a "confirmation." The faith of the fathers had got lost in its passage from the "depths" to the "heights" of society, from the pious little community of Jews in the provinces to the big city. As Kafka wrote to his father: "At bottom the faith that ruled your life consisted in your believing in the unconditional rightness of the opinions of a certain class of Jewish society, and hence actually, since these opinions were part and parcel of your own nature, in believing in yourself. Even in this there was still

Judaism enough, but it was too little to be handed on to the child; it all dribbled away while you were passing it on." During Hermann Kafka's first years in Prague, he attended the Pinkas Synagogue, where the old rituals were still followed and where Kafka too was "incomparably more impressed by the Judaic tradition," as he recalled. Later, the father switched his allegiance to the "liberalized" Altneu Synagogue, the religious center for the well-to-do Jewish bourgeoisie; Kafka speaks of "its muffled stock-exchange murmurings."

All this was quite in keeping with the Kafkas' social advancement and is further documented by the frequent changes in the family's address. In 1896 they moved from the Minuta House to the somewhat more comfortable apartment at Zeltnergasse 3, where until 1906 the father's business was also located. In that year he moved his store diagonally across the street to number 12. Finally in 1912, the fancy-goods store was established on the ground floor of one of the showplaces of the Old City, the Kinsky Palais, on whose top floor was the *Gymnasium* from which Kafka had been graduated a decade earlier.

After his graduation Kafka took his first extended trip by himself, to the German North Sea islands of Norderney and Helgoland, resorts then in fashion in Prague. (Kafka's father had visited Norderney shortly before with two of his brothers.) Upon his return, he had to decide what studies to pursue at the university. Chemistry was his initial choice, and he stuck to it (with his friends Oskar Pollak and Hugo Bergmann) for all of two weeks before he settled on law, though he continued to attend lectures in art history as well. In the summer semester of 1902 he took only classes in German language and literature and in art history; and then, because he disagreed with the thoroughly nationalistic approach of August Sauer, the senior professor of German studies, he and his school friend Paul Kisch planned to continue German studies in Munich, but eventually this plan was abandoned.

Instead, in the winter of 1902–1903 he returned to legal studies, and from then on took courses in Roman civil law, the law of inheritance, canon law, international law, legal history, civil action, criminal law, modern civil law, national and constitutional law, medical jurisprudence, political economy, financial law, philosophy of law, commercial law, and statistics. It is hard to determine what exactly was the decisive factor in his choice of the law: whether it was the family's aspirations, his own resignation, or his "indifference" to the nature of his future livelihood so long as it would also allow him to write without interference. For by this time, writing had become Kafka's "principal longing." It was to Pollak that he confided his early vision of literature:

I think we ought to read only the kind of books that wound and stab us. If the book we're reading doesn't wake us up with a blow on the head, what are we reading it for? So that it will make us happy, as you write? Good Lord, we would be happy precisely if we had no books, and the kind of books that make us happy are the kind we could write ourselves if we had to. But we need the books that affect us like a disaster, that grieve us deeply, like the death of someone we loved more than ourselves, like being banished into forests far from everyone, like a suicide. A book must be the axe for the frozen sea inside us. That is my belief.

He had, in fact, already begun to write while still at the *Gymnasium;* but only a few fragments of these early writings are preserved in letters. The first important extant manuscript is the "Description of a Struggle" ("Beschreibung eines Kampfes") of 1904–1905, written while Kafka was a member of the poetry section of "The German Students' Reading and Conversation Club in Prague." It was here that he met Max Brod, who was to become his lifelong friend, promoter, and adviser. A second lifelong friendship developed during these years, with his uncle Siegfried Löwy, a country doctor in Triesch, a bachelor, fresh-air fanatic, horseman, motorcycle and auto enthusiast, and the only relative to own an extensive library (mostly German classics). It was very likely this same uncle who directed his ailing nephew's attention to the natural-health sanatoriums that were just coming into fashion. In 1903 Kafka visited Dr. Lahmann's Sanatorium at Weisser Hirsch near Dresden, Germany, and in 1905 and 1906 Dr. Schweinburg's newly completed "Sanatorium and Hydropathic Institute" at Zuckmantel in Austrian Silesia, where for the first time he experienced "that kind of intimacy with a woman (she a woman and I a boy)."

After he had passed the three required intermediate written law examinations in the autumn of 1905 (one with a mark of "good," two with "satisfactory"), there began "those several nerve-shattering months of preparation for the [final] examinations, during which I nourished myself intellectually on nothing but the sawdust that had been chewed for me by a thousand eager mouths." These examinations consisted of three oral tests known as the *Rigorosa,* and Kafka barely managed to pass them with a grade of "satisfactory." In those years, neither a dissertation nor any further written work was required.

On June 18, 1906, Kafka was "promoted" to Doctor of Law by the Imperial and Royal German Karl-Ferdinand University of Prague.

GYMNASIUM
AND
UNIVERSITY

The bar mitzvah.

Upper left. The ceiling of the Zigeuner (Gypsy) Synagogue with its stucco decorations. The building was demolished during the "sanitizing" of the ghetto.

Above. Kafka at about thirteen.

Left. Invitation from Hermann Kafka ("and wife," added by hand), sent to friends and acquaintances, announcing his son's "confirmation," according to the assimilationist custom.

Above. The Pinkas Synagogue, regularly attended by the family during their first years in Prague; photograph from the time of the "sanitizing" of the ghetto.

Left. Zeltnergasse 12, where Hermann Kafka had his place of business on the second floor from 1906 to 1912.

Opposite. Zeltnergasse 3, the "House of the Three Kings," where the Kafkas had an apartment from 1896 to 1907. Here for the first time Kafka had his own bedroom—with a view onto the street—and kept it until he completed his studies at the university. Here, too, he wrote his first works, the most important being "Description of a Struggle."

From the 1890s until 1906 the father's store, now a wholesale establishment, was in this same building, shown here in a recent photograph.

HERRMANN KAFKA, PRAG I.
Zeltnergasse 3.
Galanteriewaren en gros Geschäft.

Top. View of the staircase at Zeltnergasse 3.
Above. Hermann Kafka's business letterhead, used until 1906.
Left. Two versions of Hermann Kafka's business logo. The jackdaw, a glossy black grackle-like bird, is called *kavka* in Czech. The upper emblem shows the bird perched on a "German" oak branch; the lower one is politically more neutral.

Opposite above. The Civilschwimmschule, a bathing and boating establishment, moored alongside the bank of the Moldau. As a young boy Kafka often came here with his father. Later he kept his own rowboat here. In the middle distance, far right, is the Hradschin (Castle Hill); in the far background, the Laurenziberg (Saint Lawrence Hill).
Opposite below. The Kinsky Palais on the Altstädter Ring. From 1893 to 1901 Kafka attended the *Gymnasium* (high school) on its third floor. From 1912 on, the father's business was elegantly housed on the ground floor, right-hand corner. This photograph from the 1920s reveals that Kafka's father—under the influence of the newly founded Republic of Czechoslovakia (after World War I)—had reverted to the Czech spelling of his first name, Heřman.

41

Class photograph (1898), with school director Frank (left) and head master Emil Gschwind (right). Kafka is second from left in the top row. His friends: Paul Kisch (on his right), with whom he later planned to pursue German studies; Oskar Pollak (second row from top, second from left), his closest friend until he entered the university; Rudolf Illowý (third row from top, far left), with whom he discussed socialism; Hugo Bergmann (third row from top, third left), a Zionist; Ewald Felix Přibram (third row from top, far right), an atheist, also a very close friend. *Below.* The earliest known example of Kafka's handwriting, an entry in Hugo Bergmann's friendship album (1898). "We come and we go, and sometimes we say good-bye never to meet again."

Opposite. Two portrait photographs, taken around 1899. Below these, the Laurenziberg as seen from the Hradschin. "I was sitting once on the slope of the Laurenziberg. I was mulling over what I wanted my life to be. My most important, or most enthralling, desire, it seemed, was to achieve a view of life in which it would both retain its own normal, ponderous fall and rise, but at the same time be perceived as a nothingness, a dream, a hovering in air."

Nr.	Name	Geburtsort	Geburts-Tag und Jahr	Dauer der Gymnasial-studien, Jahre	Grad der Reife	Gewählter Beruf
1	Becking Wilhelm	Prag	15. März 1882	9	reif	Militär
2	Bergmann Hugo	Prag	25. Dec. 1883	8	reif mit Auszeich.	Jurisprudenz
3	Ehrenfeld Samuel	Gnesen	25. Feber 1883	8	reif	Kaufmann
4	Fischer Paul	Prag	15. Sept. 1881	8	reif	Maschinen-bau
5	Flammer-schein Oskar	Prag	14. Juni 1883	8	reif	Handels-wissenschaft
6	Gibian Camill	Karolinen-thal	3. Sept. 1883	8	reif	Jurisprudenz
7	Hecht Hugo	Prag	23. Juli 1883	8	reif	Medicin
8	Heindl Alexander	Turnau	20. März 1881	9	reif	Handels-wissenschaft
9	Jeiteles Alois	Neuern	17. April 1881	9	reif	Medicin
10	Kafka Franz	Prag	3. Juli 1883	8	reif	Philosophie
11	Kisch Paul	Prag	19. Nov. 1883	8	reif	Philosophie
12	Kraus Karl	Prag	12. Feber 1883	8	reif	Philosophie
13	Patz Victor	Hohenelbe	13. Juli 1882	8	reif	Medicin
14	Pollak Hugo	Prag	11. März 1882	8	reif	Jurisprudenz
15	Pollak Oskar	Prag	5. Sept. 1883	8	reif	Chemie
16	Přibram Ewald	Prag	11. Jan. 1883	8	reif	Chemie
17	Stein Victor	Zbirov	13. März 1881	9	reif	Bodencultur
18	Steiner Karl	Theresien-stadt	15. Aug. 1881	8	reif mit Auszeich.	Eisenbahn-dienst
19	Steininger Anton	Nehasitz	13. Juni 1881	8	reif	Jurisprudenz
20	Steuer Otto	Prag	11. Jan. 1881	9	reif	Philosophie
21	Strauss Otto	Prag	17. Oct. 1883	8	reif	Philosophie
22	Utitz Emil	Prag	27. Mai 1883	8	reif mit Auszeich.	Philosophie

Above left. Kafka as a *Gymnasium* graduate (1901). *Above right.* The names of the "successful candidates for graduation," in the annual report of the Altstädter Gymnasium.

Below. The North Sea resort of Norderney in a panoramic drawing of the period, showing its principal tourist attraction, the recently constructed "sea walk" jetty. In the summer of 1901, following his graduation, Kafka took his first long trip alone, to the islands of Norderney and Helgoland.

Above.   Kafka's father (right) on Norderney, around 1900. His brother Ludwig, a merchant and later an insurance agent in Prague, is at the left with his wife, Laura. Another brother, Filip, a merchant in Kolin, is at center with his wife, Klara; she was the model for Klara Pollunder in Kafka's novel *Amerika*.

Below.   Helgoland, around 1900, as seen from the bathing beach on the mainland.

Above. The Fruit Market in Prague. In the background, the German Theater. To its right, the Karolinum (marked X), which housed the law-school lecture halls of the Imperial and Royal German Karl-Ferdinand University, where Kafka enrolled as a law student in the autumn of 1901.

Below. Although not completely authenticated, this was probably Kafka's writing table when he was a student. In any case, it was found among the family's possessions. To the right, an advertisement for the first Austrian bicycle in series production, manufactured by Puch's First Styrian Bicycle Factory, Inc., founded in 1900.

A servant gave the following description of Kafka's room at Zeltnergasse 3 in 1903: "His room was simply furnished. Next to the door was a writing table on which lay the Roman law in two volumes. Opposite the window was a wardrobe, in front of it a bicycle; then the bed; next to the bed a nightstand; and by the door a bookcase and a washstand."

„PUCH-RAD"

Feinste Präcisions-Strassenmaschine

Above. The sociologist Alfred Weber, at the time a member of the Prague University law faculty. He was designated as Kafka's doctoral adviser.

Right. Horaz Krasnopolski, professor of civil law and a central figure in legal studies at Prague. As examiner in the oral law finals (the *rigorosa*), he was a man much feared by Kafka as well as others.

Below. Photograph of the University of Munich in the early 1900s. In October 1902 Kafka came here to explore the possibility of pursuing German studies. The plan was quickly abandoned.

Das Schloss.   Die Schule.

Gruss aus Triesch!

Above. Picture postcard sent by Kafka to his oldest sister, Elli (eleven at the time), from Triesch, July 22, 1900. Triesch is a village near Iglau in Moravia (recent photograph *below*) where Kafka's favorite uncle, the country doctor Siegfried Löwy, lived and practiced. Kafka visited him again in 1902 and frequently thereafter.

Right. Dr. Siegfried Löwy.

Below. The marketplace in Triesch, in a recent photograph. The doctor's home and practice were in the house at center right. "I am riding around on the motorcycle a good deal, swimming a lot, lying nude in the grass by the pond for hours, hanging about the park until midnight with a bothersomely infatuated girl, have already tedded hay in the meadow, have set up a merry-go-round, helped trees after a storm, taken cows and goats to pasture and driven them home in the evening, played a lot of billiards, taken long walks, drunk a lot of beer, and I have even been in the temple too."

49

Above. At Uncle Siegfried's. Flash picture dated December 7, 1914. Siegfried standing, second from left. Kafka's sister Ottla seated, second from left. On either side of her, Trude and Martha Löwy, daughters of Uncle Richard from Prague. On the wall, a photograph of an automobile.

Below. Siegfried's house. The open entry in front led to the stable, later converted into a garage. (Recent photograph.)

Above. Hedwig Weiler. Kafka met her in Triesch in 1907.
Right. View from Uncle Siegfried's living-room window, in a recent photograph.

Below right. Motorcycle built in 1903 by the Laurin & Klement Company in Jungbunzlau (later the Skoda Works). Model name: "Odradek." In 1907 all vehicles in the Austro-Hungarian Empire were registered for the first time: there were 2,314 automobiles and 5,387 motorcycles, one of which was owned by Uncle Siegfried.
Below. The castle park in Triesch.

Staatsprüfungszeugnis.

Herr *Franz Kafka,*

geboren zu *Prag in Böhmen*

~~derzeit~~
zuletzt } ordentlicher Studierender der Rechts- und Staatswissenschaften

an der k. k. *deutschen* Karl-Ferdinands-Universität zu Prag hat am

23. November 1905 vor der unterfertigten Staatsprüfungskommission

sich in Gemäßheit des Gesetzes vom 20. April 1893, Reichs-Gesetz-Blatt Z. 68,

und der Ministerial-Verordnung vom 24. Dezember 1893, Nr. 204 R.-G.-Bl., der

judiciellen

Staatsprüfung unterzogen und dieselbe

mit *genügendem* Erfolge

bestanden.

Von der k. k. Staatsprüfungskommission

Prag, den *23. November 1905*

Präses der Kommission.

Prüfungskommissäre.

Abstufung der Kalkule:

I.	II.	III.	IV.
gut mit Auszeichnung	gut	genügend	nicht genügend

52

The degree of Doctor of Law required the successful completion of three qualifying examinations: in history of law, jurisprudence and political science. The certificate *at left* states that Kafka passed the jurisprudence examination with a grade of "satisfactory."

After completing his examination in history of law, Kafka entered a sanatorium for the first time. Beginning in the summer of 1903 he felt "increasingly not altogether healthy." Presumably on the advice of Uncle Siegfried, he chose Dr. Lahmann's Sanatorium (pictured *above*) in Weisser Hirsch near Dresden, the best-known and most fashionable "natural health cure institute" of its day.

Above right. A row of the "sun-and-air cabins," which particularly appealed to Kafka. He subsequently made a point of choosing sanatoriums with these facilities.
Right. The "Fresh Air and Sun Bath."

Above. The first lines (epigraph) of the 1904 manuscript, "Description of a Struggle."

> *And the people in their finery*
> *Walk unsteadily over the gravel*
> *Under the enormous sky*
> *Which, from hills in the distance,*
> *Arches over to distant hills.*

Left. Max Brod, Kafka's lifelong friend.
Below. Lecture hall in the "Reading and Conversation
Club for German Students in Prague." Kafka and Brod
were members of its poetry section.

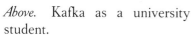

Above. Kafka as a university student.

Right. Kafka with bowler hat and collie, 1906/1908. Beneath this is the complete photograph, provided by Max Brod, showing the waitress Hansi Julie Szokoll.

Below. Kafka as a student with his "Madrid uncle," Alfred.

Opposite. Recent photographs of Dr. Ludwig Schweinburg's Sanatorium and Hydrotherapy Institute in Zuckmantel. *Top,* general view. *Center,* main building and social center. *Bottom,* ruins of the "water-cure" installation and a view from the sanatorium. Kafka spent several weeks here during the summers of 1905 and 1906. He writes delightedly to Brod that he has "become rather lively." Later he confessed that in Zuckmantel he had experienced for the first time "that kind of intimacy with a woman (she a woman and I a boy)" whom he had loved so much that it "shook me to the core." A number of details in "Wedding Preparations in the Country" refer to this place and this affair.

Right. Kafka as a young university student.
Below. Tourist advertisement for the town of Zuckmantel and a general view of this Austrian-Silesian community.

Zuckmantel (Österr.-Schlesien)

Sehr malerisch, 416 m ü. M., nächst der Bischofskoppe. Bewald. Berge, markierte Wege, ausged. Promen., herrl. Aussichtspunkte u. Naturschönheiten. Station. Fernspr., mod. Gas- u. elektr. Beleucht. Sanatorium u. Wasserheilanstalt, Sommerfrische, gut. Wasser. Wallfahrtsort Mariahilf, zugängl. gemachte Ruine Edelstein. Schutzh. Rudolfsheim a. d. Bischofskoppe m. Kaiser-Franz-Joseph-Aussichtswarte, reizende Fern- u. Rundsicht. — Auskünfte v. Stadtvorstand, Sudetengebirgsverein, Verein z. Hebg. d. Fremdenverkehrs.

Kafka as a Doctor of Law,
around 1906.

Name, Alter und Geburts-ort des Candidaten. Name und Charakter des Vaters. Datum des Absolutoriums.	Rigorosum I. Aus dem römischen, kanonischen und deutschen Recht.	Rigorosum II. Aus dem österreichischen Civilrecht, Handels- und Wechselrecht, österreichischen Civilprocess und österr. Strafrecht.	Rigorosum III. Aus dem allgemeinen und österr. Staatsrecht, dem Völkerrecht und der politischen Oekonomie.	Datum der Promotion und Name des Promotors.
Franz Kafka geb. am 3. Juli 1883 zu Prag in Böhmen, Sohn des Hermann K Kaufmannes Abs. Prag 3¹/₇ 1905	Am 13. Juni 1906 das Rigorosum wurde mit aller Stimmen für genügend erklärt.	Am 7. November 1905 das Rigorosum wurde mit zwei von einer Stimmen für genügend erklärt.	Am 16. März 1906 das Rigorosum wurde mit seiner fünf Stimmen für genügend erklärt	Am 18. Juni 1906 Promotor: Prof. Weber

Above. Transcripts from 1905–1906, the years in which Kafka took and passed his three oral examinations *(rigorosa)*. His "promotion" is dated June 18, 1906.

FRANZ KAFKA BEEHRT SICH ANZUZEIGEN, DASS ER AM MONTAG DEN 18. JUNI D. J. AN DER K. K. DEUTSCHEN KARL FERDINANDS-UNIVERSITÄT IN PRAG ZUM DOKTOR DER RECHTE PROMOVIERT WURDE.

PRAG, IM JULI 1906.

Right. Announcement of his degree, sent to friends and acquaintances.

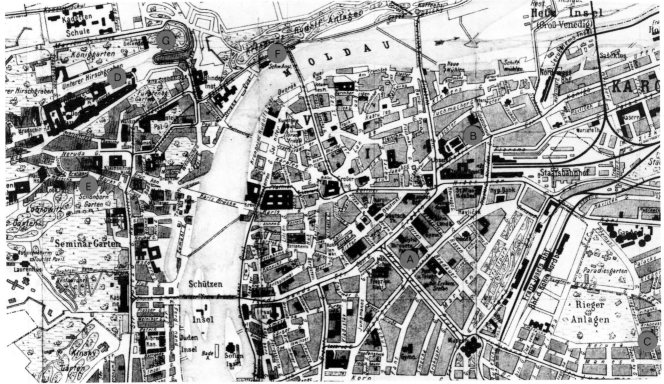

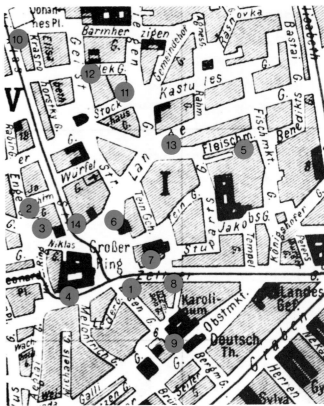

A. The Assicurazioni Generali, Kafka's place of work, 1907–1908.
B. The Workers Accident Insurance Company, where Kafka worked from August 1908 until his "retirement" in June 1922.
C. Nerudagasse 48 (sister Elli's apartment), Kafka's temporary address from September 1914 to January 1915.
D. Alchimistengasse 22 (sister Ottla's apartment), where Kafka wrote from November 1916 to April 1917.
E. The Schönborn Palais, where Kafka lived from March to August 1917.
F. The Civilschwimmschule, a public place for swimming and boating.
G. The Chotek Park and its belvedere, Kafka's favorite place in Prague.
1. The Smetana House on the Altstädter Ring, where Kafka's mother lived with her parents before she was married.
2. Location of house (no. 30/I) where Kafka's father lived before his marriage. Demolished in 1897–1898.
3. Kafka's birthplace, no. 27/I. Only the entryway still stands.
4. The Minuta House, where the family lived from 1889 to 1896.
5. The *Volksschule* (grammar school) on the Fleischmarkt, which Kafka attended from 1889 to 1893.
6. The Kinsky Palais. Kafka's *Gymnasium* (1893–1901) was located on its third floor; from 1912 on, his father's business was on its ground floor.
7. Zeltnergasse 3, the family's residence from 1896 to 1907; during most of this period the father's store was also located here.
8. Zeltnergasse 12, the father's place of business from 1906 to 1912.
9. The Karolinum, site of the University Law School, which Kafka attended from 1901 until he received his Doctor of Law degree in 1906.
10. Niklasstrasse 36, the family's residence from June 1907 to November 1913.
11. The Café Savoy, corner of Stockhausgasse and Ziegengasse, where the Yiddish acting company performed.
12. Bilekgasse 10. From August into September 1914 Kafka lived here in his sister Valli's apartment.
13. Lange Gasse 18 (today no. 16), "House of the Golden Pike," Kafka's residence from March 1915 to February 1917.
14. The Oppelt House, Altstädter Ring 6 (today no. 5), the family residence from 1915 on.

Prague, Capital of the Kingdom of Bohemia

Prague, the third largest city of the Austro-Hungarian Empire after Vienna and Budapest, had about half a million inhabitants at the turn of the century, if we include the population in its outlying suburbs. The central city itself contained about 140,000 people and was divided into five distinct districts: the Kleinseite, or Little Town, on the west bank of the Moldau (Prague III), with the Castle District of the Hradschin (Prague IV); on the east bank, within the bend of the river, the Josefstadt, the former ghetto (Prague V), surrounded by the Altstadt, or Old City (Prague I), which in turn was bounded on the southeast by the Neustadt, the New City (Prague II).

By Kafka's time more than 90 percent of the population was Czech. In 1900 no more than 34,000 inhabitants designated themselves as German-speaking, and of these half came from among Prague's 25,000 Jews. This German element was concentrated in the city's nucleus, the Altstadt and the Josefstadt, comprising almost a quarter of its 40,000 residents. The strong though not predominant presence of "Germans" in the center of the city did, however, correspond to the existing power structure; it was evidence of their still valid claim to the top rungs of the social ladder, not only in financial matters but in cultural ones as well. They could still boast two theaters, two daily newspapers, a major university, an institute of technology, and (as social emblem and focal point) the German Casino on the Graben, Prague's principal avenue.

On the other hand, beginning in 1883 (the year of Kafka's birth) the Czechs managed to obtain a majority in the State Parliament despite the notorious *Zensus-wahlrecht,* a bill of enfranchisement based on skewed census figures, which discriminated against them. From 1891 on, all street signs were in Czech. In the same year the Bohemian Exposition took place, an important event for the nascent Czech national consciousness; two cable tramways and the observation tower atop the Laurenziberg (Saint Lawrence Hill) were specially built for this occasion.

In 1893, following violent nationalistic turmoil, Vienna declared a state of emergency and enforced it for two years. Nevertheless, unrest broke out again in 1897, this time with anti-Semitic overtones, the so-called December Storm. From then on the members of the Jewish middle class were, as Theodor Herzl describes them, "like powerless stowaways attempting to steer a course through the storms of embattled nationalities."

During the following decade the government was basically run by a series of emergency decrees, interrupted by the violent agitation for universal suffrage. In one dramatic instance, the Prague Social Democrats under Soukup organized a demonstration on the Altstädter Ring in November 1905 with more than 200,000 participants. At the same time, an antinationalistic approach was taken both by the republican Realist Party led by the future founder of Czechoslovakia, Thomas Masaryk, and by a small group of Anarchists under Neumann and Kacha. (Kafka was interested in all three organizations.)

In 1913 the central government in Vienna abolished the autonomy of the Kingdom of Bohemia on the grounds that its parliament was no longer able to function. In October 1918, at the end of World War I, the Republic of Czechoslovakia was proclaimed with Prague as its capital.

During all the years he lived in Prague, Kafka hardly ever ventured out of the inner city, except to leave town altogether. The Minuta House, his grammar school and *Gymnasium,* the various business addresses of his father, the university, the apartments in the Zeltnergasse and Niklasstrasse, the Oppelt House, his office—all these places were located in the Old City within a radius of little more than a hundred yards. An acquaintance remembers Kafka saying, as they looked down from a window at the Altstädter Ring: "Here was my *Gymnasium;* there in that building peeking out at us was the university; and a little farther to the left, my office. This little circle [and he drew a couple of small circles with his finger] encompassed my entire life."

It was precisely during Kafka's lifetime that the physical appearance of the inner city was transformed more radically than at any other time before or since. Everywhere, the old three- and four-story buildings were demolished and replaced by new ones in the pompous "Vienna style." The most dramatic transformation, however, was accomplished by the nearly total demolition of the former ghetto, which in Kafka's youth had been a Mecca for junk dealers, whores, drunks, and the downtrodden "little folk." During the two decades after 1893, the entire area was rebuilt, or to use the euphemism of the day, "sanitized." On the site of "three hundred wretched houses" there rose "eighty-one apartment palaces," in several of which the Kafka family lived from 1907 on. Fifteen years later Kafka said to Gustav Janouch, the author of *Conversations with Kafka:*

In us all it still lives—the dark corners, the secret alleys, shuttered windows, squalid courtyards, rowdy pubs, and sinister inns. We walk through the broad streets of the newly built town. But our steps and our glances are uncertain. Inside we tremble just as before in the ancient streets of our misery. Our heart knows nothing of the slum clearance which has been achieved. The unhealthy old Jewish town within us is far more real than the new hygienic town around us.

PRAGUE

Above. Model of the Old City made by Anton Langweil between 1826 and 1834. Easily identifiable are Kafka's birthplace (X) and two of the family's later addresses, the Minuta House (+) and Zeltnergasse 3 (O). *Below.* "Sanitizing" the ghetto, about 1905.

Above. The Zigeunergasse (Street of Gypsies), before "sanitizing."

Above. A street for prostitutes (1902).

Below. The Altneu (Old-New) Synagogue before the "sanitizing." (Old photograph.)

Below. The Altneu Synagogue and behind it the Jewish Town Hall after the "sanitizing." (Recent photograph.)

The Graben, Prague's main thoroughfare. Upper picture, around 1890, with horse-drawn streetcars. Lower picture, around 1905, with electric streetcars. In the background, the Powder Tower. At the center of the upper photograph is the Café Continental and, in the building immediately in front of it, the Café Central, both frequented by Kafka. *Opposite above.* The ghetto in 1890. *Below.* Wenzelsplatz (Saint Wenceslaus Square), 1890.

Above. Stereoscopic panorama of the Hradschin seen across the Moldau, about 1900. *Opposite.* View from the left bank of the Moldau to the Mühlenturm (Water Mill Tower) and the Altstädter Brückenturm (Bridge Tower) on the Old City side. *Below.* Promenade along the Franzensquai on the right bank, 1893.

Bridges over the Moldau. *Top.* The Emperor Franz Bridge, leading across the river from the Kleinseite (left bank) of the Moldau via the Schützeninsel (island with poplars) to the National Theater on the right bank. *Above.* The Emperor Charles Bridge (begun 1357), Prague's oldest. The Hradschin is in the right background. *Opposite above.* The Kettensteg, a pedestrian chain bridge, from the Rudolfinum to the Kleinseite. *Opposite below.* The Emperor Franz Josef Bridge (or Empress Elisabeth Bridge) with its streetcar line to the Baumgarten Park on the Kleinseite. Tollkeeper's booth at right.

Above left. The Emperor Franz Josef Station, 1907, decorated for the emperor's reception. *Right.* Emperor Franz Josef in Prague, 1907. *Below.* Altstädter Ring with the Clock of the Apostles (left) and Týn Church (center).

Above left. Acrobats performing at the Folk Art Exposition in 1895.
Above right. Prague's first "Edison Phonograph Salon," at the Jubilee Exposition in 1891.
Below. The Fruit Market, around 1910.

Above. A downtown beer parlor.
Below. A chestnut vendor.

Above. A pushcart coffee vendor, around 1910.
Below. A "sanitary facility" with a public scale.

Above. Hydraulically powered cable railway from the Franz Josef Bridge to the Belvedere Plateau, 1891.
Below. One of the first motion-picture houses, the Royal Bioskop in Žižkov, 1911.

Above. V. Jelínek's "Steam and Dry Cleaning" establishment, 1908.
Below. In a coach and wagon shop in Prague-Libeň, 1913.

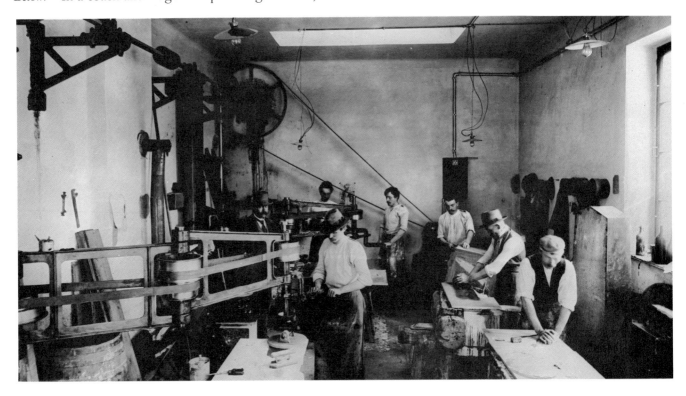

Above.   Cement factory in Podol near Prague, around 1900.   *Below.*   Headquarters of the *Prager Tagblatt,* a Prague daily paper, Herrengasse 16. Also in the Herrengasse was the Grand Hippodrome, where Kafka took riding lessons.

Above. Horse-drawn streetcar at the Kreuzherrenplatz terminus of the tramway, around 1901. *Below.* A "saloon car" of the electric tramway standing in front of the Clock of the Apostles, 1913. At left, the Minuta House.

Above. A group of drivers at a coach stand in Prague, around 1910.
Below. A prostitute stepping from a "Green Tony" (the Prague term for a prison van) around 1905.

View of Kafka's favorite walk in Prague. In the foreground, the road to the Chotek Park. In the background, the Hradschin and Cathedral, the Metropolitan Church of Saint Vitus, begun 985. To the right, in front of the castle, the freestanding round tower called the Daliborka, at the end of the Alchimistengasse. Ottla had rented a little house on this street for Kafka, and he worked there in 1916–1917.

Trips, Friendships, Family Relations

Kafka was a city dweller, with the corresponding enthusiasm of such people for the outdoors, for unspoiled nature, fresh air, and the healthy life. The line which divided Prague from the surrounding countryside was well defined in Kafka's day, and close by. There were open fields right beyond Smichov and Liben. Podbaba, Troja, Libotz, and Kuchelbad were still small villages, easily reached by streetcar in less than an hour. Other places such as Stechowitz on the Moldau, Liboch on the Elbe, or Radotin, Černošice, Dobrichowitz, and Karlstein, all on the Beraun River, made for agreeable day trips. Until the last year of his life, Kafka made repeated excursions to two of them in particular, Dobrichowitz and Liboch.

Much as Kafka preferred to take short walks alone, he desired companionship on longer excursions and on trips far from home. On such occasions his favorite companions were his lifelong friend Max Brod and, less often, the philosopher Felix Weltsch and the writer Oskar Baum, both of whom Kafka had come to know through Brod and with whom he had continued to attend lectures and discussions in Prague ever since their days together at the university.

Relatives, too, frequently provided the occasion for trips away from home; hardly any of Kafka's numerous uncles and aunts lived in Prague. Filip, his father's oldest brother (whose family appears in various guises in the novel *Amerika*), was a merchant in Kolin; Heinrich, another paternal uncle, was a merchant in Leitmeritz. Two aunts, Anna and Julie, Hermann's sisters, lived in Strakonitz, not far from the paternal village of Wossek. Uncle Siegfried, a brother of Kafka's mother, was a country doctor in the Moravian town of Triesch. Kafka visited all these relatives numerous times, even his maternal uncle, Josef Löwy, a wholesale import grocer in Paris. The only one missing from the long list of family hosts is the mother's eldest brother, Alfred, the "Madrid uncle," but Kafka met him, too, on his frequent visits back to Prague.

On these visits to relatives, summer holiday trips, and day excursions, and especially on his many business trips, Kafka got to know the towns and the changing landscape of Bohemia very well indeed. He covered most of the country from Kuttenberg to Karlsbad, from Friedland to Strakonitz, and from Pilsen to Trautenau.

Moreover, for someone living at that time in the relatively provincial city of Prague, with only the rare opportunities for vacation trips available to a hardworking official, Kafka saw a good deal of Europe and was witness to a number of the technological advances of his day. In Germany, he knew the Baltic and North Sea coasts, the Harz Mountains, the cities of Dresden, Munich, Leipzig, and Weimar; in Italy, the north Italian lakes and the cities of Trieste, Venice, Verona, Brescia, and Milan; in Switzerland, the area around Lake Lucerne, Lugano, and Zurich. He visited Hungary, including Budapest, twice. Yet except for Vienna, he saw practially nothing of Austria, the principal country of the Austro-Hungarian Empire.

But he did often get to Vienna and the two other major continental capitals, Paris and Berlin, especially Berlin. Apart from the usual tourist attractions in these cities, it was the latest scientific and technological advances that claimed his curiosity and interest: the telephone, the dictating machines or "parlographs," the early cinematograph, the subway train, the automobile and motorcycle. In this connection Kafka was more of a "contemporary" than almost all his colleagues. In 1909 he cut short a vacation in Riva, in northern Italy, in order to witness an "aeronautical meeting." His description of it is the first account of these "machines" to appear in German literature. A few years after its introduction the "electric coach" also makes an appearance in Kafka's prose, as does, in 1906, the automobile: at the time a few dozen of these monsters were roaring through the streets of Prague.

Arriving in Paris in 1911 from the "hellish clamor" of Stresa (where a blacksmith's shop near the hotel had driven him frantic), Kafka managed to forget for a whole week his notorious sensitivity to noise in that far from quiet city. There is not a word about this otherwise omnipresent topic in his travel diaries. The life of the great city was simply too fascinating—this "rushing traffic," "this placid and pleasing feeling of speed."

TRIPS, FRIENDSHIPS, FAMILY RELATIONS

84

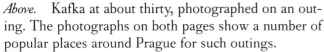

Above. Kafka at about thirty, photographed on an outing. The photographs on both pages show a number of popular places around Prague for such outings.

Opposite. Dobrichowitz on the Beraun River *(top)* and Stechowitz on the Moldau *(bottom left),* two of the villages Kafka and his friends often chose for their excursions. The Pension Stejskal in Dobrichowitz *(bottom right),* on a postcard to Felice, May 3, 1915. The picture at top, taken from a bridge, was described by Max Brod: "We were filled with the animation and happiness of summer vacationers and were hardly overjoyed at having to say to ourselves that in two days we'd be back at our desks. . . . My friend picked up a small stone and threw it over the bridge railing."

This page, right, top to bottom. Černošice on the Beraun. The Elbe at Roztok. View of the Pension Stejskal, on a card to Milena, September 5, 1923. Liboch on the Elbe.

Right. Max Brod, a drawing by Lucian Bernhard, 1909.

Left. Max Brod, a lithograph by Willi Novak; how it came about is described by Kafka in his diary, December 23, 1911.

Below left. Ufergasse 8, first house on the left, where Brod lived from 1913. In the distance, the Niklasstrasse.
Below right. Schalengasse 1; Brod lived here with his family prior to his marriage in 1913.

Above, left to right. The blind author Oskar Baum (1883–1941). The philosopher Felix Weltsch (1884–1964). Weltsch's home at Gemsengasse 4 in the Old City. Besides Brod, these were Kafka's closest friends.

Right. A trio of amateur musicians: Weltsch (center) with his friends Bergmann (left) and Süssland. Bottom row, left: Weltsch's sister Betty.

Below. The Sophieninsel (Sophia's Island), with bridge to the right bank of the Moldau. Kafka often played tennis at this popular Prague meeting place.

Studio portraits of the Kafka family, made at the photographic studio of Schlosser-Wenisch in the autumn of 1910, most likely on the occasion of the two elder sisters' wedding announcements.

Above left. Julie Kafka at the age of fifty-four.
Above right. Hermann Kafka at the age of fifty-eight.
Opposite, clockwise from upper left. Franz, age twenty-seven; Elli (Gabriele), age twenty-one; Ottla (Ottilie), age eighteen; Valli (Valerie), age twenty.

In December 1912 Kafka sent this photograph of himself to his fiancée, Felice Bauer, with the comment: "I really don't have such a twisted face, and that visionary expression comes only from the photographer's flash. I stopped wearing high collars long ago. On the other hand, the suit I'm wearing is the same one I've often mentioned before, my only suit ('only' is naturally an exaggeration, but not by much), and I'm still wearing it, as cheerfully as ever. It is growing old along with me."

Above left. Kafka's sisters in an earlier photograph (Valli, Elli, Ottla). Their governess, Marie Werner, was in the Kafkas' employ for decades and was always called simply "Fräulein"; *center,* in a photograph taken in Kuchelbad, 1919; *right,* in Prague.

Below. Elbeteinitz, Marie Werner's home village, which Kafka and Ottla once visited.

Above left.   The castle in Strakonitz and, beneath it, Castle Strahl near Strakonitz. This town was also the home of Aunt Anna, the father's sister, of whom no photograph exists; she was the widow of the owner of a match factory. *Above right.*   Aunt Julie, another paternal aunt, wife of a merchant in Strakonitz. In the summer of 1905 Kafka visited these aunts with his mother and sisters and also toured Castle Strahl.

Below.   Leitmeritz. Uncle Heinrich Kafka's store was near the marketplace (*right*); after his early death in 1886 the business was run by his widow, Karoline (*left*), who had "always been a most agreeable person" in Kafka's estimation. He visited her frequently.

Above.   The marketplace in Kolin with the statue of the Bohemian religious reformer Johannes Hus, by Franti-šek Bilek, a monument much admired by Kafka.

Left.   Filip Kafka, the father's oldest brother, a success-ful merchant in Kolin. As the family's "merry uncle," he was famous for his off-color jokes and his elegant dress. Three of his sons emigrated to America, one of them, Franz, at the age of sixteen; another son, Otto, made a considerable fortune in the new country.

Below.   Kolin as seen from the banks of the Elbe.

Recent photographs taken in Kolin. Today the visitor will find the old houses in the ghetto unoccupied, the wrought-iron doors of the shopping street barred, and the synagogue (*below right*) closed. The gravestones of Filip Kafka and his wife, Klara, however, still stand in the overgrown Jewish Cemetery outside town (*right*).

Far left. The bachelor uncle Alfred Löwy, the mother's oldest brother and director of a Spanish railroad company. He was a regular visitor to Prague, where he advised his nephew Franz on business matters.

Near left. Uncle Rudolf Löwy, Siegfried's brother, also a bachelor; he was bookkeeper for a brewery near Prague and a convert to Catholicism. He was regarded as the "family fool." Kafka's father often compared his son to Uncle Rudolf.

Below left. A family photograph taken between 1908 and 1910. Seated: mother, father, Aunt Julie from Strakonitz. Standing: Uncle Siegfried from Triesch and Uncle Richard with his wife, Hedwig.

Below right. Another picture of Uncle Richard, a clothing merchant in Prague.

Above.   Kafka's parents, around 1912, and a view of the original interior of the father's store.
Below.   The Kinsky Palais, which housed the father's store (ground floor, right corner) from 1912 on.

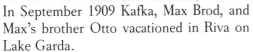

In September 1909 Kafka, Max Brod, and Max's brother Otto vacationed in Riva on Lake Garda.

Above. Kafka (right) and Otto in a snapshot taken by Max Brod.

Right. Two views of Riva.

Below. The clock tower in Brescia, a photograph from the "Kaiserpanorama," an elegant amusement arcade in Friedland, northern Bohemia, which featured stereopticon views from all over the world.

Italy's first international "Flight Meeting" was held in Brescia September 5–13, 1909. Kafka visited it with the Brod brothers. Kafka's report, "The Aeroplanes of Brescia," published in the Prague newspaper *Bohemia,* is the first account in all of German literature of these "apparatuses."

Top right, in oval. Louis Blériot, who had just flown across the English Channel, flies past the grandstand. The main photograph shows, in right foreground, the Curtiss Flyer in which Glenn Curtiss went on to win the "Grand Prize of Brescia" with a fifty-kilometer flight in forty-nine minutes, twenty-four seconds.

Center right. Rougier making his world-record altitude flight, 198 meters. In the foreground, the signal mast and judges' platform. Next to it, a Pirelli Tire banner.

Bottom right. Rougier and his flying machine.

Below. A plan of the airfield and the beginning of Kafka's newspaper report. (See Appendix.)

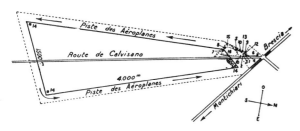

Die Aeroplane in Brescia.

Von Franz Kafka (Prag).

Wir sind angekommen. Vor dem Aerodrom liegt noch ein großer Platz mit verdächtigen Holzhäuschen, für die wir andere Aufschriften erwartet hätten, als: Garage, Grand Büfett International und so weiter. Ungeheure in ihren Wägelchen fettgewordene Bettler strecken uns ihre Arme in den Weg, man ist in der Eile versucht, über sie zu springen. Wir überholen viele Leute und werden von vielen überholt. Wir schauen in die Luft, um die es sich hier ja handelt. Gott sei Dank, noch fliegt keiner! Wir weichen nicht aus und werden doch nicht überfahren. Zwischen und hinter den Tausend Fuhrwerken und ihnen entgegen hüpft italienische Kavallerie. Ordnung und Unglücksfälle scheinen gleich unmöglich.

In August and September 1911 Kafka and Brod went on vacation to Lugano, Switzerland, by way of Zurich and Lucerne. They visited Gandria, the Villa Carlotta in Cadenabbia on Lake Como, and then traveled on to Milan, Stresa on Lake Maggiore, and finally Paris.

Left, top to bottom.   Zurich. Lucerne. Lugano (their hotel, the Belvedere, is on the point at center). Gandria.

Above.   The Villa Carlotta.

Below.   The Duomo (Cathedral) in Milan; at the left, the entrance to the Galleria Vittorio Emanuele.

Bottom.   Stresa on Lake Maggiore.

On his return trip from Paris in September, Kafka stayed for a week at a natural-health spa near Zurich, the Erlenbach Sanatorium. He remarks with some irritation "that as a result of 'naturopathy' and everything connected with it, a new type of human seems to have come into being" one that "treats its health as if that were itself an illness."

Above left. The salon of the sanatorium, with Herr Fellenberg-Egli, the owner, in the lounge chair.
Above right. The dining hall.
Right. One of the fresh-air cabins.
Below. General view from Lake Zurich.

Kafka visited Paris twice, in October 1910 and September 1911, each time for about a week.

Above. View over the rooftops toward Sacré-Coeur. Kafka called it "a city of lines and cross-hatchings."

Left. Georges Seurat's *Cirque,* at the time in the Louvre. A direct inspiration for Kafka's story "Up in the Gallery."

Below. Boulevard des Capucines. In the foreground, a "tricycle" like the one involved in a traffic accident to which Kafka devotes pages in his travel journal.

Two paintings that particularly impressed Kafka in Paris.

Right. Jean Huber's *The Levée of Voltaire at Ferney* (Musée Carnavalet). Brod describes how fascinated Kafka was by the painting's depiction of direct inspiration, the way in which Voltaire, "having just gotten out of bed and thrusting one leg into his trousers, stretches out his hand and eagerly, consumed by his ideas, immediately begins to dictate to his secretary."

Below. Adolf Roehn's *Napoleon's Bivouac on the Battlefield of Wagram, during the Night of July 5 to 6, 1809* (Versailles). Kafka notes in his diary during a visit to Versailles: "Napoleon sits alone, one leg propped up on a low table. Behind him, a smoking campfire. The shadows cast by his right leg and the legs of his chair and table radiate from him like spokes. The generals in their remote semicircle gaze into the fire and at him."

A passport photograph, taken at the time Kafka began working for the Workers Accident Insurance Company.

The Workers Accident Insurance Company

After receiving his doctorate, Kafka completed the *Rechtspraxis,* a kind of legal internship required of all law students intending to enter the civil service. It consisted of two half-year apprenticeships, one at a civil court and the other at a criminal court. It was during this time at the latest, however, that he decided not to work in the civil service or in a law office, and consulted with his uncles Siegfried and Alfred about his professional prospects. At first, he toyed with the idea of further study at the Export Academy in Vienna; but then, through his Uncle Alfred's connections, he was offered a job at the Prague branch office of the Italian insurance company Assicurazioni Generali. He described his days in a letter:

My life is completely chaotic now. At any rate I have a job with a tiny salary of 80 crowns and an infinite eight to nine hours of work; but I devour the hours outside the office like a wild beast. Since I was not previously accustomed to limiting my private life to six hours, and since I am also studying Italian and want to spend the evenings of these lovely days out of doors, I emerge from the crowdedness of my leisure hours scarcely rested.

Am in the office now. I am in the Assicurazioni Generali and have some hopes of someday sitting in chairs in faraway countries, looking out of the office windows at fields of sugar cane or Mohammedan cemeteries. . . .

I don't complain about the work so much as about the sluggishness of swampy time. The office hours, you see, cannot be divided up; even in the last half hour I feel the pressure of the eight hours just as much as in the first. Often it is like a train ride lasting night and day, until in the end you're totally crushed; you no longer think about the straining of the engine, or about the hilly or flat countryside, but ascribe all that's happening to your watch alone, which you continually hold in your palm.

The difficult working conditions at the Assicurazioni, however, soon prompted Kafka to look for another position. After a course in workers' insurance at the Prague Commercial College and with the backing of the father of his schoolmate Přibram, he was taken on by The Workers Insurance Company for the Kingdom of Bohemia in Prague on July 30, 1908.

This company had been set up as a half-private and half-state institution in 1891, following the example of social reform established by Bismarck in Germany. Its function was to represent the workingmen's newly attained rights to accident insurance and compensation. By 1908, however, the implementation of these rights had fallen far short of success. Rather, as Kafka wrote in a report, "the company seemed to be little more than a dead body, whose sole sign of life was its growing deficit." The principal cause of this, he continued, was "the grievous evasions" by factory owners and other employers, a bad situation further exacerbated by the insurance company's thoroughly inadequate methods of inspection, all of which led to a change in directorship during the first year of Kafka's employment. A young academician, Dr. Robert Marschner, became the new director. The period immediately following his appointment was marked by violent clashes with employers who sought, through protest and litigation, to fight the classification of their factories in higher-risk categories.

It was just at the beginning of these events that Kafka entered the firm. He was quickly recognized as a "superb administrative talent" and an excellent student of the law. His position entailed the formulation of "recourses" against the petitions filed by employers; the drafting of policy and publicity material for the company in connection with, for example, compulsory insurance for building trades, automobile insurance, and accident prevention; the representation of the company in court; and the inspection of factories located in the four "chief district magistracies" assigned to him in the northern Bohemian industrial area around Reichenberg.

This region, with its extensive and interconnected rail network, had developed into one of the most important industrial centers of the Danube Monarchy under "the friendly aegis of its aristocratic landowner, Count Clam-Gallas." Its factories (predominantly textile, glass, and machinery) had been built for the most part "out in the green fields" and had "their own electrical illumination by dynamo" long before the majority of other communities could even begin to think of such amenities.

These factories grew at an astounding rate. The Ginzkey Carpet Factory in Maffersdorf, for example, which began in 1847 with six looms, employed 230 workers by 1861 and 1,200 thirty years later. Klinger's woolen mills in Neustadt, which began as a cottage industry in 1844 with 600 laborers, had "two fully developed factories with 3,200 employees" by 1904. The owners' ascent on the social ladder was just as dramatic. The founders had all been modest craftsmen; their sons lived in extravagant villas adjoining their factory buildings and, for the most part, had already been "granted their patents of nobility by His Majesty."

Nothing in this success story, however, had effected a change in practices. The brutal forms of competitive capitalism remained securely in place. It was Kafka's task to deal with the physical and medical consequences of this exploitative ethic. But his observations were not just material for his files: through the many trips he took for his insurance company he came to know the inner workings of these factories intimately. He was the only "bourgeois" writer of his time who had such first-hand knowledge.

"How modest these men are," Kafka once said to Brod about the workers crippled through negligence. "They come to us and beg. Instead of storming the company and smashing it to little pieces, they come to us and beg."

THE WORKERS
ACCIDENT
INSURANCE
COMPANY

Above. View of the Zeltnergasse, 1893. In the right foreground, at the corner of the Fruit Market, is the *Landesgericht* (the high court of Bohemia), where Kafka completed his one-year legal internship, 1906–1907.

Left. The headquarters of the Assicurazioni Generali on the Wenzelsplatz. Kafka worked for this private insurance firm from October 1907 to July 1908.

Opposite. Kafka's employment application for the Assicurazioni Generali, together with the obligatory handwritten curriculum vitae. This is one of the last examples of Kafka's cursive handwriting. From 1907 on, he used only Roman script. (See Appendix.)

VERWALTUNGS-ZWEIG

Anstellungsgesuch.

K. K. PRIV.

ASSICURAZIONI GENERALI

| Eingetragen unter Nr. .... |
| Angenommen unter Nr. .... |
| Abgelehnt unter Nr. .... |

An die _Generalagentschaft_ des „_Assicurazioni Generali_" in Triest

in _Prag_

Der Unterzeichnete beehrt sich hiemit ein Gesuch um Verleihung einer Stellung bei dieser Anstalt einzureichen und gibt zugleich nachstehend alle seine Person und seine Befähigungen betreffenden, erforderlichen Angaben, unter Beischluss der entsprechenden Beilagen.

Für den Fall, dass sein Gesuch genehmigt werden sollte, erklärt der Unterzeichnete, sich den bestehenden oder einzuführenden Reglements für die Beamten, Agenten und sonstigen Functionäre der Anstalt, sowie alle jenem für die Versorgungscasse zu unterwerfen, und verspricht namentlich:

a) jede Arbeitszutheilung oder Beschäftigung anzunehmen, welche die Direction oder die Gesellschafts-Vertretung, der er zugetheilt ist, ihm jetzt oder später zuweisen sollte;

b) genau die jetzt bestehenden oder später einzuführenden Amtsstunden einzuhalten;

c) wenn der Dienst es erfordern sollte, Arbeiten auch in aussergewöhnlichen Stunden, ohne Anspruch auf besondere Entlohnung vorzunehmen;

d) sich von einer Agentur der Anstalt zu einer anderen, schon bestehenden oder erst einzurichtenden Agentur versetzen zu lassen.

Der Unterzeichnete erklärt ferner die bestehenden Regeln zu kennen, wonach:

1. Die Angestellten der Gesellschaft ausschliesslich für dieselbe thätig sein müssen, und keine Nebenbeschäftigung, kein Amt oder Ehrenamt aufnehmen dürfen, ohne die schriftliche Einwilligung der Direktion, die von ihr jeden Augenblick zurückgezogen werden kann;

2. das Gehalt monatlich und posticipando bezahlt wird;

3. falls nichts anderes vereinbart wurde, die Stellung eines wirklichen Beamten erst nach 12 Monaten ununterbrochener Dienstzeit in der Eigenschaft als Beamter erlangt wird, wobei die Zeit, in welcher er als Eleve, Praktikant oder Diurnist beschäftigt wird, nicht inbegriffen ist;

4. die Entlassung der Beamten, Agenten u. s. w., die noch nicht wirkliche Beamte sind, mit Kündigungsfrist von 14 Tagen, und für wirkliche Beamte mit Kündigungsfrist von 14 Tagen für jedes vollendete Dienstjahr, mit einem Minimum von 3 Monaten und einem Maximum von 6 Monaten, oder auch sofort gegen Vergütung der Kündigungsfrist entsprechenden Gehaltstheiles erfolgen kann;

5. die wirklichen Beamten ihren Dienst erst nach einer dreimonatlichen schriftlichen Kündigung verlassen können, alle anderen erst nach vierzehntägiger schriftlicher Kündigung;

6. der aus dem Dienste der Gesellschaft sei es zufolge Entlassung, sei es freiwillig scheidende Beamte, Agent u. s. w. keinerlei Provision, Rückzahlung oder Entlohnung für irgend welche Dienstleistung oder abgeschlossene Geschäfte beanspruchen kann, mit Ausnahme der bis zu seinem Dienstaustritte bereits fällig gewordenen Bezüge;

7. der Beamte, Agent etc. die Veränderungen seines Civilstandes ebenso wie die Wohnungswechsel der Gesellschaft anzuzeigen hat;

8. mit alleiniger Ausnahme der Bureau-Vorstände und der Abtheilungs-Chefs, kein Beamter berechtigt ist, in den ihm zur Benützung angewiesenen Schreibtischen und Kästen andere Gegenstände, als die der Gesellschaft gehörenden Geschäftsstücke unter Schloss zu verwahren;

9. die Beamten, die (mit oder ohne Absicht) eine absolute Verschwiegenheit über die geschäftlichen Vorkommnisse dritten Personen gegenüber nicht beobachten, und jene, deren Gehalte von gerichtlicher Execution betroffen werden, sofort entlassen, vertreten werden können;

10. Die Direction, auf Wunsch des Angestellten, ihm jedes zweite Jahr einen 14tägigen Urlaub bewilligen wird; der Zeitpunkt des Urlaubsantrittes wird von der Direction mit Rücksicht auf die Erfordernisse des Dienstes festgesetzt. Wenn die Direction in besonders berücksichtigungswürdigen Fällen einen längeren Urlaub bewilligt, so bestimmt sie gleichzeitig, ob der Beamte für die Urlaubszeit sein Gehalt ungeschmälert oder in reducirten Maasse oder gar nicht beziehen soll.

Fragen der Direction:

1. Welcher ist Ihr Name und Zuname und welche Titel besitzen Sie?

2. Wo und wann sind Sie geboren?

3. Welches ist Ihr gewöhnlicher Gesundheitszustand und welche Krankheiten haben Sie gehabt?

4. Lebt Ihr Vater? wollen Sie seinen Namen, seine Beschäftigung und seinen Wohnort angeben (eventuell sind die gleichen Angaben über den Vormund erforderlich).

Beantwortungen:

1. _JUDr. Franz Kafka_

2. _Prag 3. Juli 1883_

3. _Ausser Kinderkrankheiten immer gesund_

4. _Hermann Kafka Kaufmann Prag, Zeltnergasse Niklasstrasse 36_

5. Haben Sie Militärdienst geleistet? wenn nicht, aus welchem Grunde? waren Sie einjähriger Freiwilliger? wie verhält es sich mit Ihren eventuellen ferneren Militärpflichten? (z. B. beurlaubt, Reservist etc. bis zu welchem Jahre, in welcher Charge, unter Angabe der voraussichtlichen Waffenübungen).

6. Sind Sie ledig, verheiratet oder Witwer?

7. Wenn verheiratet, seit wann?

8. Wie heisst Ihre Frau und wie alt ist sie?

9. Wie viele Kinder haben Sie? welche sind ihre Namen und ihr Alter?

10. Welche ist Ihre Muttersprache, d. h. welcher bedienen Sie sich gewöhnlich?

11. Welche Schulen besuchten Sie und mit welchem Erfolge?

12. Kennen Sie ausser Ihrer Muttersprache noch andere Sprachen? Welche? Wie weit reichen Ihre Kenntnisse darin? Können Sie diese Sprachen blos verstehen oder auch sprechen, oder sich ihrer auch schriftlich bei Übersetzungen und Aufsätzen bedienen?

13. Haben Sie sich, ausser den Schulstudien, privaten Studien gewidmet? welchen Studien? Wie weit sind Sie in diesen Studien fortgeschritten?

14. Haben Sie Stenographie gelernt? können Sie sie praktisch verwenden? In welchen Sprachen?

15. Welche Stellungen hatten Sie bisher? bei welchen Privatpersonen, Instituten, oder bei welchem öffentlichen Amte? Wollen Sie die Zeit des Antrittes dieser Stellungen, ihre Dauer und den Grund des Austrittes angeben.

16. Welche Reisen haben Sie gemacht? In welchen Ländern haben Sie sich aufgehalten?

17. Wie sind Ihre gegenwärtigen Vermögens-Verhältnisse? Auf welche andere Einkünfte können Sie ausser dem Gehalte, den von Ihnen gewünschten Anstellung verbundenen rechnen?

18. Sind Sie mit einem Director, Verwaltungsrath, Vertreter, Beamten oder Agenten der Anstalt bekannt oder verwandt? mit wem? In welchem Grade?

19. Welche Personen können über Sie Auskunft ertheilen?

20. Auf wessen Empfehlung stellen Sie dieses Gesuch?

21. Wo ist Ihre Wohnung gelegen? (Strasse, Nummer).

NB. Der Bewerber wird ersucht, auf der nächsten Seite in kurzen Zügen sein curriculum vitae niederzuschreiben.

In _Prag_ den 2ten _Oktober_ 19 17

Gesehen von Vater oder Vormunde des minderjährigen Bewerbers:

Unterschrift des Bewerbers:

Dr. Franz Kafka

5. _militärfrei wegen Schwäche_

6. _ledig_

10. _deutsch_

11. _die deutsche Volksschule bis zur 4ten Klasse, dann das deutsche Staatsgymnasium, dann die deutsche Karl-Ferdinands-Universität ..._

14. _deutsche Stenographie_

15. _vom 1. April bis 1. Oktober 1906 Concipient bei Dr. Richard Löwy Obstgasse Prossnitz Ring, vom 1. Okt. 1906 bis 1. Okt. 1907 Aushilfskraft beim Landesgericht in Prag_

16. _Oesterreich, Deutschland_

17. _meine Eltern erhalten mich bisher_

18. _Herr Weißberger (Madrid)_

20. _auf Empfehlung des Herrn Weißberger Nikolstrasse 36_

NB. Die Antworten müssen durch glaubwürdige Documente bekräftigt werden. Zu 1—2 ist der Taufschein oder Geburtsschein, zu 6—9 sind die Auszüge der Magistrats-Matrikel, zu 11 die Schulzeugnisse, zu 15 die vom Chef beim Austritt aus dem Amte erlassenen Zeugnisse beizulegen. Zur Antwort 12 sind je nach den Umständen, entweder Abschriften, oder Uebersetzungen, oder Aufsätze in denjenigen Sprachen einzureichen, die der Bewerber zu kennen angibt.

CURRICULUM VITÆ.

Ich bin am 3. Juli 1883 in Prag geboren, besuchte die Altstädter Volksschule bis zur 4ten Klasse, dann in das Altstädter deutsche Staatsgymnasium; mit 18 Jahren begann ich meine Studien an der deutschen Karl-Ferdinands-Universität in Prag. Nachdem ich die letzte Prüfung absolviert hatte, trat ich am 1. April 1906 als Concipient bei einem Advokaten Dr. Richard Löwy Altstädter Ring ein. Im Juni legte ich das historische Rigorosum ab und wurde im selben Monate zum Doktor der Rechte promoviert.

Ich war, wie ich es mit dem Herrn Advokaten auch gleich vereinbart hatte, in die Kanzlei nur eingetreten um die Zeit bis zum ... zu nützen, denn schon von Anfang hatte ich die Absicht, nicht bei der Advokatur zu bleiben. Am 1. Oktober 1906 trat ich in die Rechtspraxis ein und blieb dort bis zum 1. Oktober 1907.

Prager Handels-Akademie.
Kurs für Arbeiter-Versicherung.

Zeugnis.

Herr Dr. Franz Kafka,

geb. zu Prag in Böhmen

hat in der Zeit vom 3. Februar bis 20. Mai 1908,
den infolge Erlasses des k. k. Ministeriums für Kultus und Unterricht vom 12. Mai 1908,
Z. 17.808, an der **Prager Handels-Akademie** errichteten **Kurs für Arbeiter-Versicherung** besucht und erhält über den Fortgang nachstehendes Zeugnis.

Leistungen in den einzelnen Unterrichtsgegenständen:

Entwicklung der Arbeiter-Versicherung in den europäischen Staaten und in Österreich insbesondere. Allgemeine Rechtsbestimmungen der Unfallversicherung. Entschädigungsagenda derselben. Bruderladenversicherung.	vorzüglich	Dg. Dr. Marschner
Einnahmsagenda der Unfallversicherung (Versicherungspflicht, Einreihung der Betriebe, Beitragsleistung und Kontrolle). Statistik.	vorzüglich	E. Pfohl
Spezielle Rechtskunde der Krankenversicherung (Versicherungspflicht, Organisation und Detailbehandlung des Kassawesens).	vorzüglich	Dr. Fleischmann
Buchhaltung a) Grundbegriffe der einfachen und doppelten Buchhaltung b) Buchhaltung bei der Kranken- und Unfallversicherung	vorzüglich	O. Laasch

Prag, am 11. Juni 1908.

Der Direktor der Prager Handels-Akademie:

Th. Ried

k. k. Regierungsrat.

PRAGER HANDELSAKADEMIE

Notenskala.
Vorzüglich, lobenswert, befriedigend, genügend, nicht genügend.

Der ergebenst Gefertigte bittet den löblichen Vorstand der Arbeiter-Unfall-Versicherungsanstalt für das Königreich Böhmen um gütige Aufnahme als Hilfsbeamter und unterstützt diese Bitte mit Folgendem:

Die beigeschlossenen Staatsprüfungszeugnisse und das Absolutorium erbringen den Nachweis, dass der Petent an der k. k. deutschen Karl-Ferdinands-Universität in Prag die drei Staatsprüfungen mit Erfolg abgelegt hat.

An dieser Universität hat er auch nach Ablegung der drei Rigorosen am 18. Juni 1906 den juridischen Doktorgrad erlangt.

Vom 1. April 1906 bis zum 1. Oktober 1906 war Petent als Advokatursconcipient tätig, trat dann in die Gerichtspraxis ein, in der er bis zum ersten Oktober 1907 blieb und ist seitdem Beamter der k. k. priv. Assicurazioni Generali in Prag.

Der Petent ist der deutschen und böhmischen Sprache in Wort und Schrift mächtig, beherrscht ferner die französische, teilweise die englische Sprache. Er hat vom 3. Februar d. J. bis zum 20. Mai den Kurs für Arbeiterversicherung an der Prager Handelsakademie besucht und die Prüfungen laut beigelegten Zeugnisses abgelegt.

Im Jahre 1906 war Petent bei der dritten Stellung und ist militärfrei.

Prag, am 30. Juni 1908

J. U. Dr. Franz Kafka

Right and above. The headquarters and official seal of the Workers Accident Insurance Company for the Kingdom of Bohemia in Prague, at Pořič Strasse 7. Kafka's office was on the top floor. He worked here from 1908 until his retirement in 1922.

Opposite left. Kafka's certificate from the Prague Handelsakademie (commercial college), where he completed a course in workmen's insurance at the same time he was employed by the Assicurazioni Generali. His teachers there, Robert Marschner and Eugen Pfohl, were later to become his superiors.

Opposite right. Kafka's petition to the "worthy Board of Directors" of the Workers Accident Insurance Company for employment. (See Appendix.)

Above. The main stairwell and a corridor in the Workers Accident Insurance Company building.
Below. The Josefsplatz in 1907, which Kafka crossed daily on the way to his office. *Opposite.* A street-front café on the Josefsplatz, at the corner of the Pořič Strasse, on which Kafka's company was located.

Above. Dr. Otto Přibram, chairman of the board of the company.

Left. Evaluation of Kafka's performance at work, on a confidential "qualifying report" filled out by his immediate supervisor, Eugen Pfohl, the head of the technical division, after Kafka had worked there for some ten months. Pfohl attests to "a very high degree of diligence and a persevering concern in every category." Kafka, he writes, has been active "in the interests of the firm outside working hours," and Pfohl has "gotten to know the abovementioned employee as an outstanding junior officer."

Near right. Dr. Robert Marschner, the director of the company, with his daughter.

Far right. One of Kafka's few book reviews, a report on Marschner's technical study of maternity insurance in the monthly journal *Deutsche Arbeit* (German Work), June 1910.

erschaftsverficherung vom Standpunkte der ungswissenschaft« von Dr. Robert Marsch= ektor der Arbeiter-Unfall-Versicherungs-Anstalt ent der technischen Hochschule in Prag.

: Schrift, einem Sonderabdruck der „Zeit= vie gesamte Versicherungswissenschaft" (Berlin, · Sohn), liegt eine wissenschaftliche Grund- Mutterschaftsversicherung vor, also die wissen= Grundlegung eines in seiner Gänze noch Problems, dessen Dringlichkeit vielen gestern inziges sicheres Merkmal schien. Während iesem Thema bei uns außer einer in dieser ig verarbeiteten teils agitatorischen, teils nur Literatur dem näher Interessierten nichts stand, was über jene Grenzen hinaus ge= te, sind in dieser Schrift alle über ganz verstreuten Ansätze einer Mutterschaftsver= ter einem Blick vereinigt, der gleich gerecht dem menschlichen wie dem wissenschaftlichen roblems und gleich besonnen gegenüber dem vie dem noch zu leistenden Teil der Aufgabe. wahrhaftigen organisatorischen Umsicht ist iele Zwecke gesorgt: die Agitation erhält iche Kräftigung, die Wissenschaft übersichtliches r weiteren Beobachtung, aber nicht nur die sondern auch die Legislatur und Judikatur ollen; nur die private Versicherung scheint m sozialem Gefühl allerdings, zu eilig aus der Mutterschaftsversicherung gewiesen. Doch nmittelbare Wirkung auf die Allgemeinheit ergessen: die Gleichgültigen werden erweckt, Gewonnenen in eine gute Richtung gebracht leicht möglich, daß diese Schrift für die ´versicherung viel mehr bedeuten wird, als

Below. The office of a typical business firm in Prague around 1912.

Above.   The first telephone exchange in Prague, 1895; and a standard telephone of 1910.
Below.   An illustrated excerpt from a piece written by Kafka concerning accident insurance for wood-planing machine operators; from the annual *Report of the Workers Accident Insurance Company for the Kingdom of Bohemia in Prague and Its Activities.* (See Appendix.)
Opposite.   Worker in a carbide factory (*top*), and workers at a textile-glazing machine (*bottom*), both around 1910.

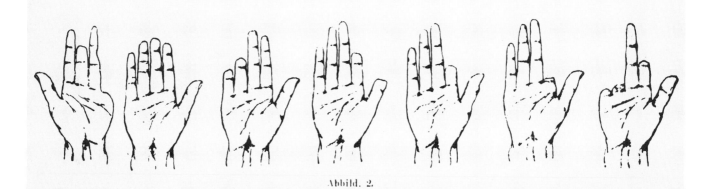

Abbild. 2.

Aber nicht nur alle Vorsichtsmassregeln, auch alle Schutzvorrichtungen schienen dieser Gefahr gegenüber zu versagen, indem sie sich entweder als durchaus ungenügend erwiesen, oder zwar einerseits die Gefahr verminderten (im Wege selbsttätiger Zudeckung der Messerspalte durch Schutzblechschieber oder durch Verkleinerung der Messerspalte), andererseits aber die Gefahr erhöhten, indem sie den Spähnen keinen genügenden Fallraum gaben, so dass die Messerspalte sich verstopfte und häufig Verletzungen von Fingern vorkamen, wenn der Arbeiter die Spalte von Spähnen freimachen wollte.

Reichenberg. Wienerstraße.

Reichenberg, the center for the industrial production of textiles, machinery, glass, and wood products in northern Bohemia, was the most important of four provincial administrative districts that Kafka, as a junior officer of his insurance firm, had under his supervision and whose factories he inspected on many business trips. The other districts were Friedland, Rumburg, and Gablonz.

Opposite:

Upper left. On these trips Kafka stayed at the Hotel Eiche in the Wiener Strasse.

Upper right. Reichenberg's theater, which Kafka frequently attended.

Center right. Reichenberg's city hall.

Bottom. The largest of Reichenberg's factories, the woolen mills of Johann Liebieg.

The industrialist Liebieg was the first person to undertake an extended automobile tour: in 1894, he drove from Reichenberg to Mannheim, Germany, in 69 hours. In 1907 he founded the Reichenberg Automobile Factory. *Right,* two of his 1909 models, a touring car and a limousine. *Below,* interior view of one of Liebieg's spinning mills.

Left.　Maffersdorf, on a postcard to Ottla, 1909.
Center left.　The Ginzkey Carpet Factory in Maffersdorf in 1858, and its founder, Ignaz Ginzkey.
Center right.　Interior and (*bottom*) general view of the Ginzkey factory, 1898.
Opposite:
Top.　The woolen mills of Ignaz Klinger in Neustadt on the Tafelfichte River, about 1890.
Center.　The worsted mills of Anton Richter's Sons in Raspenau-Mildenau, 1902.
Bottom.　View of the valley of the Elbe near Aussig, on a postcard to Felice, April 22, 1913.

Left and above. The Old Market, city center, and "American skyscrapers" in Gablonz on the Neisse River, the center of the Bohemian glass industry.
Below. Report in the *Gablonzer Zeitung* for October 2, 1911, of a talk given by "the Concipist Dr. Kafka," including an account of the "bitter complaints" lodged by the manufacturers about the excessive premium payments expected of them, inadequate lobbying in parliament, and the "surprise attacks" on their factories by trade inspectors.

Arbeiter-Unfallversicherungsanstalt.

§ Ueber das Wesen der Unfall-Versicherung sprach am Donnerstag Abend im Hotel Geling auf Veranlassung des Vorstandes der Gewerbe- und Handelsgenossenschaftsverbandes der Konzipist der Prager Arbeiter-Unfallversicherungsanstalt Herr Dr. Kafka. Redner verbreitete sich zunächst über das Unfall-Versicherungspflicht im allgemeinen und besprach dann diejenige der kleingewerblichen Motorbetriebe, vornehmlich der Gürtlereien. Längere Zeit verweilte Redner bei der Ausfüllung des Fragebogens zur Einschätzung in die Gefahrenklassen für Kleinbetriebe und bezeichnete die genaue Ausfüllung dieser Fragebogen als unbedingt notwendig, sie liege sowohl im Interesse des Gewerbetreibenden wie in jenem der Unfallversicherungsanstalt. Groß sei die Zahl der Klagen über die Einreihung in die Gefahrenklassen und doch werde hierbei seitens der Anstalt mit größter Gewissenhaftigkeit vorgegangen. Wohl könnten bei der oft mangelhaften Ausfüllung der Fragebogen, wie bei der in dem kurzen Zeitraume von nur einigen Monaten zu erfolgenden Einreihung von rund 37.000 Betrieben in die einzelnen Gefahrenklassen Mißverständnisse vorkommen, aber niemals eine absichtliche stärkere Belastung dieses oder jenes Gewerbetreibenden. Bei den kleingewerblichen Motorenbetrieben werde auch auf die Intensität des Motorbetriebes Rücksicht genommen. Infolge der mangelhaften Ausfüllung der Fragebogen mache sich jetzt eine öftere Aussendung derselben notwendig, damit die Anstalt endlich einmal in die Lage komme, die richtige Gefahrenklasse für die Einreihung der einzelnen Betriebe zu ermitteln. Vorläufig sei nach dieser Richtung hin das Gutachten des Gewerbeinspektorates maßgebend. Eine Besichtigung der Betriebe sei leider noch nicht vorgeschrieben und deshalb müsse man sich auf den Gewerbeinspektor verlassen. Für die Gürtlereien empfahl Redner den Abschluß der Versicherung aufgrund der nicht unbedeutende Vorteile bietenden Pauschalierung, und gab im Namen der Anstalt das Versprechen, daß in diesem Falle allen berechtigten Wünschen nachgekommen werden würde. Ein Fehler sei es noch, daß die Arbeiter-Unfallversicherungsanstalt mit ihren Mitgliedern in einem nur sehr notdürftigen Verkehre stehe, auch die Korrespondenz sei sehr trübseliger Art und die Jahresberichte würden nicht beachtet. Dieser Zustand sei kein guter und liefere nicht den Boden, den die lebendige Institution brauche. Die Anstalt strebe selbst mit allen Kräften danach, ein anderes Verhältnis zwischen sich und den Mitgliedern herzustellen. Anstalt und Mitglieder seien doch eigentlich eins. Aber es herrsche eine gewisse Animosität gegen die Anstalt. Das solle anders werden. Ein reger Verkehr zwischen Anstalt und Mitgliedern sei vor allem nötig und werde von der Anstalt angebahnt. Die Reorganisation des Kontrolldienstes solle erfolgen und Sorge getragen werden, daß die Kontrolle nicht mehr so plötzlich vorgenommen werde. Jeder Neueinreihung in die Gefahrenklassen würden künftig Unterhandlungen mit den Unternehmern vorausgehen. Schon bei der letzten Neueinreihung hätten solche Unterhandlungen zu guten Resultaten geführt. Schließlich sei auch geplant, seitens der Anstalt in Fachzeitschriften über Gesetzesauslegungen und sonstige die Anstalt betreffende Fragen zu berichten. In der diesem Vortrage folgenden Debatte führte Herr Franz Tandler bittere Klage über die Einreihung der Wagner in eine so hohe Gefahrenklasse. Anfänglich hätte diese Gewerbegruppe auf je 100 Kronen anrechenbare Lohnsumme 1·98 K, später 2·15 K gezahlt und jetzt betrage der Beitrag über 4 K für 100 K anrechenbare Lohnsumme. Wohl hätten einige Genossenschaftsmitglieder gegen diese Einreihung den Rekurs ergriffen; aber ohne jeden Erfolg und die Ablehnung sei eine schablonenmäßige gewesen. Motorenbetrieb wäre in der Wagnerei wenig zu finden, meistens würde Handarbeit geliefert. Die Beitragserhöhung sei einzig und allein auf das Gutachten des Gewerbeinspektorates zurückzuführen. Es zeige sich eben überall, daß dem Gewerbestande eine ausreichende Vertretung im Abgeordnetenhause fehle. Nur die mangelhafte Vertretung der Gewerbetreibenden im Parlamente trage die Schuld an dem Zustandekommen gewerbefeindlicher oder das Gewerbe schwer belastender Gesetze. Redner will durchaus nicht den Gewerbeinspektoren zu nahe treten, die wohl theoretisch sehr gut vorgebildet seien, aber praktisch bleibe viel zu wünschen übrig. Es sei auch gar nicht möglich in allen gewerblichen Betrieben bewandert zu sein. Auf alle Fälle gehörten auf solche verantwortungsvolle Posten praktische Fachleute. Das Laienhafte der Gewerbeinspektoren zeige sich sehr oft an der Anordnung von Schutzvorrichtungen an Maschinen, die den Betrieb geradezu hindern und von den Arbeitern sehr oft während der Arbeit beseitigt werden müßten. Gedanken und Augen bei der Arbeit, das sei der beste Schutz gegen jeden Unfall. Herr Kammerrat Max Boperschalek stimmte den Ausführungen des Vorredners zu, bezüglich der unzureichenden Vertretung des Gewerbestandes im Parlament. Ueber die Gewerbeinspektoren seien auch bei der Handels- und Gewerbekammer schon wiederholt Klagen laut geworden. Besonders riefen die Ueberrumpelungen der Gewerbetreibenden seitens der Gewerbeinspektoren überall Mißstimmung hervor. Der Fabrikant wie der Gewerbetreibende könnten verlangen, daß eine Inspektion ihrer Betriebe in ihrer Anwesenheit erfolge und dazu sei die vorherige Anmeldung des Gewerbeinspektors notwendig. Herr Roman Palme bezeichnete die vom Gewerbeinspektor mitunter angeordneten Schutzvorrichtungen eher für gefahrbringend als gefahrabwendend. Die weiteren Redner Herren Rudolf Tham, Ignaz Pokora, Siegmund Hiebel, Ferdinand Hirschmann, Julius Schläger und Rafael Hütter kritisierten in oft scharfer Weise das Vorgehen der Unfallversicherungsanstalt. Letzterer beschwerte sich über die langsamen Erledigungen von Rekursen seitens der Anstalt und zeigte an einem Beispiele wie minimal die von der Anstalt bewilligten Unterstützungen bei Unfällen seien, sie stünden in keinem Verhältnis zu den Einzahlungen. Schließlich wurden von allen Seiten Beschwerden über die Kontrollorgane der Anstalt geführt. Herr Dr. Kafka versprach, alle Beschwerden der Direktion der Anstalt zu unterbreiten, die gewiß zu einer eingehenden Prüfung derselben bereit sein würde. Die weiteren Redner Herren Rudolf Tham, Ignaz Pokora, Siegmund Hiebel, Ferdinand Hirschmann, Julius Schläger und Rafael Hütter kritisierten in oft scharfer Weise das Vorgehen der Unfallversicherungsanstalt. Der Obmann des Genossenschaftsverbandes Herr Stadtrat Johann Rößler, der den Vorsitz in der Versammlung führte, dankte am Schlusse derselben Herrn Dr. Kafka für seinen aufklärenden Vortrag und hofft, daß die Versammlung, welcher Vertreter aller Gewerbegenossenschaften und des Gewerbevereines beiwohnten, zur Besserung des Verhältnisses zwischen den Gewerbetreibenden und der Arbeiter-Unfallversicherungsanstalt beigetragen haben möge.

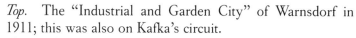

Top. The "Industrial and Garden City" of Warnsdorf in 1911; this was also on Kafka's circuit.

Above. Postcard to Ottla, April 1911, with "greetings from the Warnsdorf Health Food Restaurant." The other, more recent photographs on the page show the factories and villas of Warnsdorf industrialists.

In January and February 1911 Kafka made an extended business trip to Friedland in northern Bohemia.

Above. Hydroelectric works.
Left and below. The castle, "an extensive complex" in the possession of Count Clam-Gallas. (Earlier it had belonged to the great General Wallenstein, duke of Friedland.) It became one of the models for Kafka's novel *The Castle.* Note the substantial difference between the tourist postcard view (*left*) and the way Kafka would have seen it, from the vantage point of an insurance official inspecting the Wilhelm Siegmund textile factory (*below*), huddled at the foot of the castle promontory.

Above left. View of the marketplace in Friedland as seen from Kafka's hotel window.

Above right. One of the stereopticon photographs in the "Kaiserpanorama" collection, "the sole entertainment in Friedland." Shown here is a tomb monument described in Kafka's travel journal.

Right. Factory building on the banks of the Wittig River, in a recent photograph.

Below left. View of the "Cottage Quarter" near the train station, a typical company-owned workers' settlement; these generally had their own restaurants, pubs, and community houses.

Below right. A privately owned worker's house.

Above. View of Prague from the Belvedere Plateau, 1911. On the right, the Emperor Charles Bridge and, in front of it, the suspended Kettensteg, a pedestrian chain bridge that was torn down and replaced by the Maneš Bridge soon after this picture was taken. The Týn Church (with scaffolding) is at center. At left, the Čech Bridge, completed in 1908. By this time, the old ghetto buildings had been completely replaced by modern structures. Clearly visible (X) is the corner building at Niklasstrasse 36, where the Kafkas lived (top-floor apartment) from June 1907 to November 1913. Here Kafka wrote "The Judgment," *Amerika,* and "The Metamorphosis."

Left. Passport photograph, 1911–1912.

The Year 1912

"This constant, overriding anguish; if only I had gone away in 1912, in full possession of all my energies, with a clear head, not gnawed to bits by the exhausting attempts to suppress my vital energies!" This diary entry from December 1915 is one of many remarks by Kafka in which he looks back to the year 1912 as the turning point in his life.

Until that year, as he writes in *Letter to His Father*, he had "grown up rather like a businessman who goes about his daily life with worries and forebodings, to be sure, but who doesn't keep a precise tally of it all." What Kafka was attempting to explain to his father in the business terminology familiar to him had to do, of course, with literature or, to be more precise, with life as a writer. This was the choice that confronted him in 1912, after almost five years of professional life as an official of the Workers Accident Insurance Company.

For two years Kafka had been regularly keeping a

diary in which again and again short prose pieces crop up, as well as the beginnings of longer texts. In the winter of 1911–1912 he writes an extensive first working version (later rejected) of what he calls "the American novel." At the end of July 1912 he discusses for the first time the possibility of a book with a publisher. Three months later, in the course of a single night, he writes "The Judgment" in his diary.

This story, "The Judgment," I wrote at one sitting during the night of the 22nd–23rd, from ten o'clock at night to six o'clock in the morning. I was hardly able to pull my legs out from under the desk, they had got so stiff from sitting. The fearful strain and joy, how the story developed before me, as if I were advancing over water. Several times during this night I heaved my weight on my back. How everything can be said, how for everything, for the strangest fancies, there waits a great fire in which they perish and rise up again. How it turned blue outside the window. A wagon rolled by. Two men walked across the bridge. At two I looked at the clock for the last time. As the maid walked through the anteroom for the first time I wrote the last sentence. Turning out the light and the light of day. The slight pains around my heart. The weariness that disappeared in the middle of the night. The trembling entrance into my sisters' room. Reading aloud. Before that, stretching in the presence of the maid and saying, "I've been writing until now." The appearance of the undisturbed bed, as though it had just been brought in. . . . Only in this way can writing be done, only with such coherence, with such a complete opening out of the body and soul.

Two days after that he begins to write—again in his diary—the second version of the opening of *Amerika*. And in November and December he begins and completes "The Metamorphosis."

The beginning of this productive period was marked by Kafka's encounter with a Yiddish acting company from Poland that performed in Prague for several months beginning in October 1911. The site of these performances was Hermann's Café-Restaurant Savoy on the Ziegenplatz, where conditions could hardly have been worse, at least according to Yitzak Löwy, the leading actor in the troupe and subsequently Kafka's friend. "The stage was a corner, the audience on two sides: directly opposite us and to the left of the stage.

The curtain fell in front of us and, at the same time, on our left."

Kafka went to see this troupe of actors regularly, at least twenty times and probably much more often. In the course of his life it was the theatrical event he saw most frequently, and its influence can be detected even in his late works. Just as interesting to Kafka was the world of Eastern European Jewry, its culture and its piety, to which Yitzak Löwy also introduced him. Here, for the first time, Kafka encountered an entirely different kind of Jewish identity.

In the summer of 1912 Kafka spent a week in Weimar, almost entirely absorbed in following the traces of the great German classicists Goethe and Schiller. The trip was motivated not only by his interest in literary history but also by a personal search for his identity as a writer.

The trip to Weimar was followed by one of the most remarkable episodes in Kafka's life, his three-week "cure" at Justs Jungborn (Just's Fountain of Youth) in the Harz Mountains, a "model institute for the pure and natural way of life." Its guiding motto was "Light, Air, Mud, Water." The guests strolled naked in the "sun-and-air parks," and outside the parks dressed in "reform" (that is, health) clothing and sandals. The diet was vegetarian: "Along with various nut meats—which must be recognized as the central ingredient in human nourishment—and all kinds of native fruit, our menu consists of citrus and other imported natural fruits, milk and butter from grazing cattle as reinforcements and supplemental aids, all-natural Jungborn bread, stewed fruit, salads, potatoes, and lots of curd cheese; also pure malt-barley coffee."

The Jungborn buildings housed common rooms, a writing salon, and a hall where the proprietor regularly held forth on Nature and Christianity. Communal excursions were organized, and as a healthful and appealing diversion, "the orchards and berry patches offered the guests of the spa an opportunity for physical exercise and work"—which Kafka surely took advantage of, both here and elsewhere later in his life, just as he adhered to the Jungborn diet from this time on.

The year 1912 was also one of intense crises in the family. At the end of December 1911 the first grandchild was born (Elli had married a year earlier), a circumstance that prompted Kafka's father to "parade through the apartment in his nightshirt, throw open every door . . . and proclaim the advent of the child as if it had not merely been born, but had already lived a life full of glory and honor and then received burial."

Several days after this event, a series of clashes with the family began that lasted for years. They were centered on the "miserable" asbestos factory that Elli's husband had founded and that was supported in part by a sum of money Kafka's father had given Franz in order to make him a silent partner in the firm. The secret intent behind this move was probably to lure Kafka (despite his clear lack of talent as a businessman) into the life of commerce by way of a vaguely defined role as a roving "factory supervisor." From the moment this plot was hatched, Kafka opposed it decisively and often vehemently. The conflict led him twice to consider suicide; the second time, in October 1912 (when even his favorite sister, Ottla, took their father's side), provoked his first violent outburst of hatred against the family: "I hate them all, one after the other."

This crucial confrontation occurred precisely in the weeks of his most productive literary activity, beginning with the composition of "The Judgment" ("Das Urteil"). Just a few days previously, his sister Valli had become engaged; just a few weeks previously at Max Brod's apartment Kafka had met "the Berlin girl," Felice Bauer, his future fiancée, to whom he dedicated "The Judgment."

THE YEAR
1912

Aber jeden Tag soll mindest eine Zeile gegen mich gerichtet werden wie man die Fernrohre jetzt gegen den Kometen richtet. Und wenn ich dann einmal vor jenem Satze erscheinen würde hergelockt von jenem Satze so wie ich z. B. letztes Weihnachten gewesen bin und wo ich so weit war, daß ich mich nur noch gerade fassen konnte und wo ich, wirklich auf der letzten Stufe meiner Leiter schien, die aber ruhig auf dem Boden stand und an der Wand. Aber was für ein Boden, was für eine Wand! Und doch fiel jene Leiter nicht, so drückten sie meine Füße an den Boden, so hoben sie meine Füße an die Wand.

One of the first pages of the diary Kafka kept from 1910 on. (See Appendix.)

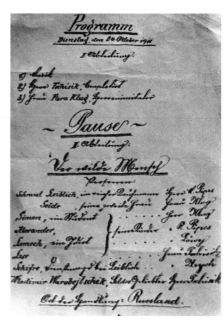

In 1911–1912 Kafka attended many performances by a touring Yiddish acting company in Prague.

Above left. Flora Klug, a male impersonator (see Kafka's diary, October 5, 1911). Yitzak Löwy (*center*) in the title role of *The Wild Man,* a play by Jakob Gordin; and (*right*) a handwritten program for the same play.

Left. Announcement for *The Wild Man* in the *Prager Tagblatt* for December 22, 1911.

Below. Recent photographs of the former Café Savoy at the corner of the Ziegengasse and the Stockhausgasse, where the Yiddish actors' troupe performed.

Above. The Yiddish dramatists Abraham Goldfaden, Jakob Gordin, and Josef Lateiner, whose plays Kafka saw performed. In his diary he writes of Goldfaden: "Married; a spendthrift even when penniless. About a hundred plays. Steals liturgical melodies and popularizes them. Everybody sings them." Of Gordin: "Better than Lateiner, Scharkansky, Feinmann, etc., because his work has more detail, more order, and more logical consistency within this order; consequently his plays don't have quite the direct, slap-dash, improvised Jewishness of the others."

Right. The Yiddish actor Yitzak Löwy, a friend of Kafka's. He told Kafka about Jewish life in Poland and brought him into contact with a wide range of Yiddish literature.

Below. Article in the Prague Zionist paper *Selbstwehr* (Self-Defense) about an "Eastern European Jewish Recitation Evening" given by Löwy in February 1912; it had been arranged by Kafka, who introduced the program with a talk on the Yiddish language. (See Appendix.)

Oſtjüdiſcher Rezitationsabend.

Sonntag, den 18. d. M. fand im Feſtsaale des jüdiſchen Rathauſes der angekündigte Rezitationsabend des Wa.ſchauer Shauſpielers Herrn J. Loewy ſtatt. Nach einer feinen und liebenswürdigen Konferenz, die Herr Dr. Kafka hielt, eröffnete Herr Loewy ſeine Darbietungen mit einigen Rezitationen, und gab in bunter Fülle Ernſtes und Heiteres, Rezitation, dramatiſche Szenen und Geſang. Es war ſehr intereſſant, dieſe oſtjüdiſchen Gedichte und Lieder, die zum Teil in Prag ſchon bekannt waren, nicht nur von einem Oſtjuden, ſondern auch ohne weſtliche Schulung zu hören. Es fiel dabei manches von den künſtleriſchen Reizen, dafür gewann alles an gewiſſermaßen hiſtoriſchem, dokumentariſchem Werte. Herr Schneller erläuterte die Texte in einer jeden Programmabſchnitt unermüdlich eröffnenden Anſprache in feiner, diskreter Weiſe. Das Publikum, zuerſt ein wenig fremdartig berührt durch die ungewohnte Sprache, kam dann doch in die richtige Stimmung und das erwünſchte Verſtändnis hinein und quittierte die Leiſtungen des Herrn Loewy mit reichem Beifall. Der Abend hat zur näheren Erkenntnis oſtjüdiſchen Weſens gewiß viel beigetragen, und Herr Loewy, der ſich als ein kräftiger und wirkungsſicherer Vortra.jener erwies, kann mit dem erzielten Eindrucke zufrieden ſein.

5323.　RUSH STREET BRIDGE, CHICAGO, ILL.

COPYRIGHT, 1900, BY DETROIT PHOTOGRAPHIC CO.

Battery, Lower End of Manhattan Island, New York.

When Kafka was working on his "American novel" *Der Verschollene* (literally, "the man who was lost without a trace" or "never heard from again"; the title *Amerika* was later given to it by Brod), his theme was very much in the air. The contacts of the Czech Anarchists (whose meetings Kafka attended) with their emigrant comrades in the United States were as intimate as those of the Social Democrats. Soukup, the Social Democrat party leader in Prague, was publishing accounts of his trip to America at the time. Kafka was not only an avid reader of such reports but was also familiar with an account of a trip to America by the social critic Arthur Holitscher. Finally, there were the Kafka-Löwy family accounts: Uncle Alfred had visited America in 1905, and between 1904 and 1909 four of Kafka's cousins had emigrated there, two of Uncle Filip's sons and two of Uncle Heinrich's.

Opposite. Two picture postcards (from Chicago and New York) sent by the "Madrid uncle," Alfred Löwy, to his parents (Kafka's grandparents), 1905.

Right. An ocean liner carrying emigrants printed as a closing vignette in Holitscher's account of America, 1912.

Below. A 1838 steel engraving of the Brooklyn Ferry, used without Kafka's approval as frontispiece by the publisher of the first edition of *The Stoker,* later incorporated as the first chapter of *Amerika.* Kafka felt "contradicted" by this old illustration, since he "had depicted the most up-to-date New York."

Weimar — Stein's Haus

Weimar — Schillerhaus

Weimar, Schloss Tiefurt.

In the summer of 1912 Kafka and Max Brod took a week's trip to Weimar, the home of the great German classicists.

Opposite:

Top. The house of Charlotte von Stein, Goethe's long-time intimate, on a card from Kafka to Ottla, July 3 (*left*). Friedrich Schiller's house (*right*).

Center. Interiors of Goethe's study (*left*) and of his garden house (*right*).

Bottom. A blurred snapshot of Kafka with the daughter of the Goethe House custodian, Margarethe Kirchner (*left*). Tiefurt Castle (*right*), which Kafka visited with the Kirchner family.

Right. Goethe's garden house (*top*) and, directly beneath, a sketch of the same building made by Kafka.

Below left. The German poet Johann Gleim's house in Halberstadt, on a postcard sent by Kafka to Brod with the observation that "these German writers certainly had it good! Sixteen windows with a view of the street! And even if the house was filled with children . . ." (In point of fact, the house has more windows than Kafka counted, and Gleim had neither wife nor children.)

Below right. One of the "special mail coaches" that took guests from the station at Eckertal to the natural-health spas in the Harz Mountains.

Halberstadt. Gleimhaus

The Jungborn (Fountain of Youth) was a large private spa in the Harz Mountains dedicated to the "natural-health way of life"—nudism, hydrotherapy, mud packs, and a vegetarian diet. Kafka spent three weeks there in July 1912. *Above left.* An advertising postcard with a picture of the founder, Adolf Just. *Above right.* One of the "sun-and-air cabins," in which one could also spend the night. Kafka esteemed these bungalows highly. *Below.* First page of the advertising brochure.

Above.   The pasture near the Stapelburg and the rise from Ilsenburg to the Jungborn, in recent photographs.

Below.   Aerial view of the Jungborn taken in the 1920s. Foreground, left of center, the main building, in which the Just family lived. To the right, a smaller administration building and the main entrance. The large complex beyond the gate housed the social rooms and dining halls. Far right, the "Fresh-Air Park" with its main building and adjoining rows of cabins. These were separated into the "Gentlemen's Park" and the "Ladies' Park," each surrounded by "high, solid plank walls." Foreground, far left, the Eckerkrug, a restaurant not part of, but managed in conjunction with, the Jungborn; it also served meat dishes.

JUNGBORN i. Harz. Partie aus dem Herrenluftpark.

138

At the Jungborn, Kafka worked on *Amerika*. He wrote Brod: "I quite like it here.... A touch of America is being pumped into these poor bodies." And: "Don't criticize the convivial life! I, too, came here for the sake of meeting people.... Look at the way I live in Prague! This need for people turns to fear as soon as it's satisfied. It's only on vacations that things turn out well."

Opposite.   Entertainments at the Jungborn. *Top,* posing for the photographer in the "Gentlemen's Park." *Center left,* the water-bucket carriers. *Bottom left,* the social center with writing room. *Bottom right,* in Imperial Wilhelminian headdress.

Above.   Mud-pack tubs and ball games.

Below.   Lining up for the "nudist crawl" or "the morning roll call."

Right.   A performance of *Echo and Narcissus* by the Dalcroze School of Dance (1912); Kafka was impressed.

Left. Wedding picture of Valli and Josef Pollak, January 1913. Kafka in background at right.

Below left. The parents with Elli, her husband, Karl Hermann (they were married in 1911), and their son, Felix, on summer holiday, 1914.

Below right. Prag Žižov, Bořivojova 27, rear courtyard; formerly the factory barracks for workers at the Prague Asbestos Works, Hermann & Co., in which Kafka had a partnership interest, but "only by dint of an investment made by my father." It was given him in compensation for the unusually large dowry bestowed on Elli. Kafka hated this factory, which did not stay in operation long and which occasioned frequent violent arguments with his parents. They had expected him to show a stronger "concern for business." In early October 1912, two weeks after Kafka's literary breakthrough with his story "The Judgment," these altercations even led him to thoughts of suicide. "I would stand at the window for long periods, and frequently I was tempted to amaze the toll collector on the bridge below by my plunge."

Grosser Lärm

Ich sitze in meinem Zimmer im Hauptquartier des Lärms der ganzen Wohnung. Alle Türen höre ich schlagen, durch ihren Lärm bleiben mir nur die Schritte der zwischen ihnen Laufenden erspart, noch das Zuklappen der Herdtüre in der Küche höre ich. Der Vater durchbricht die Türen meines Zimmers und zieht im nachschleppenden Schlafrock durch, aus dem Ofen im Nebenzimmer wird die Asche gekratzt, Valli fragt, durch das Vorzimmer Wort für Wort rufend, ob des Vaters Hut schon geputzt ist, ein Zischen, das mir befreundet sein will, erhebt noch das Geschrei einer antwortenden Stimme. Die Wohnungstüre wird aufgeklinkt und lärmt, wie aus katarrhalischem Hals, öffnet sich dann weiterhin mit dem Singen einer Frauenstimme und schliesst sich endlich mit einem dumpfen, männlichen Ruck, der sich am rücksichtslosesten anhört. Der Vater ist weg, jetzt beginnt der zartere, zerstreutere, hoffnungslosere Lärm, von den Stimmen der zwei Kanarienvögel angeführt. Schon früher dachte ich daran, bei den Kanarienvögeln fällt es mir von neuem ein, ob ich nicht die Türe bis zu einer kleinen Spalte öffnen, schlangengleich ins Nebenzimmer kriechen und so auf dem Boden meine Schwestern und ihr Fräulein um Ruhe bitten sollte.   *Franz Kafka*

Above. "A Great Commotion." (See Appendix.) In October 1912 Kafka wrote about this little vignette to his future fiancée, Felice Bauer (*right,* with her mother): "A description of the acoustic situation in our apartment. Because it was printed in a Prague magazine with a small circulation, it has managed to accomplish almost nothing by way of public chastisement of my family."

Below. View of the Kafkas' apartment house, Niklasstrasse 36 (framed by the columns). The toll collector was posted at the foot of the right-hand column.

Es war an einem Sonntagvormittag im schönsten
Frühjahr. Georg Bendemann, ein junger Kaufmann,
saß in seinem Privatzimmer im ersten Stock eines
der niedrigen, leichtgebauten Häuser, die entlang
des Flusses in einer langen Reihe fast nur in der
Höhe und Färbung unterschieden sich hinzogen. Er
hatte gerade einen Brief an einen sich jetzt im
Ausland befindenden Jugendfreund beendet,
verschloss ~~den Brief~~ ihn in spielerischer Langsamkeit
und ~~sah schaut~~ sah dann ~~nach den~~ über ~~die~~ Ellbo-
gen auf den Schreibtisch gestützt aus dem Fenster
auf den Fluss, die Brücke und die Anhöhen
am andern Ufer mit ihrem schwachen Grün.
Er dachte darüber nach, wie dieser Freund, mit seinem
Fortkommen unzufrieden, vor Jahren schon
nach Rußland sich förmlich geflüchtet hatte. Nun
betrieb er ein Geschäft in Petersburg, das anfangs sich sehr
gut ~~hatte~~ angelaufen ~~sich~~, seit langem aber schon zu stocken schien,
wie der Freund bei seinen immer seltener werden-
den Besuchen klagte. ~~Georg dagegen war in der~~
~~Heimat geblieben~~ So arbeitete er sich in der Fremde
nutzlos ab, der fremdartige Vollbart verdeckte nur
schlecht das seit den Kinderjahren wohl bekannte
Gesicht, dessen gelbe Hautfarbe auf eine sich entwickeln-

Opposite and above. The first and last pages of the original manuscript of "The Judgment," written in Kafka's diary during the night of September 22–23, 1912. (See Appendix.)

Right. Kafka's note on the back of his calling card on the morning of September 23, excusing himself for not appearing at work on time. He has had "a little fainting spell," he tells his superior, Oberinspektor Pfohl, and may not get to the office until the afternoon. (See Appendix.)

The face of the calling card sent to Pfohl on September 23, 1912, discovered in the personnel files of the insurance company: "Resumed his duties at the office today. 9.24.1912."

The First Books

Kafka began writing when he was only fifteen years old, possibly even earlier. He later burned nearly all those "many disgusting old papers." As early as 1907, when he was twenty-four and working such long hours at the Assicurazioni Generali that he hardly had time for anything else, Kafka was already speaking of writing as "this horrendous occupation; having to do without it now is my total misfortune."

That same year, Max Brod introduced Kafka to Franz Blei, an influential patron of young writers. Blei invited Kafka to collaborate with him in editing *Hyperion*, a journal financed by the celebrated author Carl Sternheim and published by the house of Hans von Weber. It was in the first issue of this journal—a publication of lavish format devoted entirely to contemporary literature and art—that Kafka first appeared in print with eight short prose pieces numbered I through VIII, collectively entitled "Meditation" ("Betrachtung").

Nearly five years went by before his first book was published. It too came about as a result of Brod's efforts. In 1912 Brod had sought out the avant-garde firm of Rowohlt in Leipzig, founded less than two years earlier by Ernst Rowohlt and his partner, Kurt Wolff. During their trip to Weimar, Brod and Kafka made a brief stopover on June 29 in Leipzig, where Brod discussed publication projects while Kafka wandered about the town. That afternoon, the two friends met at the Goethe monument and Brod took Kafka along to a tavern where Rowohlt and his readers Walter Hasenclever and Kurt Pinthus were waiting. Kafka writes: "Everyone was gesticulating with walking sticks and arms." Afterward they went to the Café Français, where Rowohlt seemed "quite serious about getting a book out of me."

This book, consisting of eighteen prose sketches set in large type and exactly one hundred pages long, appeared in November 1912 in a numbered edition of eight hundred copies under the title *Meditation* (*Betrachtung.*) The volume still bore the imprint of Rowohlt, even though he had left the firm by that time. A few months later the house changed its name to the Kurt Wolff Verlag.

Meanwhile Max Brod had also brought Franz Werfel to the publisher's attention. Wolff hired him as reader for the firm, but Werfel unexpectedly showed great activity in other areas. Of particular importance was his initiation of "Der Jüngste Tag" ("The Newest Day"*), a series of books that Wolff was able to sell at so low a price (eighty pfennigs, or less than twenty cents a volume) that it soon became the most effective instrument for the propagation of the new Expressionist literature.

Three books by Kafka appeared in this series: *The Stoker* (*Der Heizer*) in 1913, *The Metamorphosis* (*Die Verwandlung*) in 1915, and *The Judgment* (*Das Urteil*) in 1916. These were the only books of Kafka's to be reprinted during his lifetime, *The Stoker* twice, *The Metamorphosis* and *The Judgment* once each. Reliable estimates put the size of each of these printings at somewhere between one and two thousand. The modest printings alone show that Kafka (compared, for example, with Werfel or Sternheim) was indeed an

*The German phrase also connotes the Last Judgment.

"unknown" author during his lifetime. This is further corroborated by the small printings of the three other books published in his lifetime: *In the Penal Colony* (*In der Strafkolonie*) appeared in 1919 in a limited edition of one thousand, and the editions of *A Country Doctor* (*Ein Landarzt*) in 1920 and of *A Hunger Artist* (*Ein Hungerkünstler*) in 1924 were not much larger, two thousand each at most. Additional proof can be deduced from the slowness of the recorded sales. The original eight-hundred-copy edition of *Meditation*, for example, was still available eleven years after publication; the thousand-copy edition of *In the Penal Colony* was not sold out even a decade after it was first printed.

The notion that Kafka never wanted to be published and that he always had to be urged into print is a legend. On the contrary, it is well documented that he often pressed for publication, that in the case of one book—his last—he even arranged for a new publisher, and that he not only offered his work to periodicals but also carefully chose which reprint offers to accept. In a word, he was always circumspect about where he would be published.

THE FIRST
BOOKS

II Was werden wir in diesen Frühlingstagen tun, die jetzt rasch kommen? Heute früh war der Himmel grau, geht man aber jetzt zum Fenster, so ist man überrascht und lehnt die Wange an die Klinke des Fensters.

Unten sieht man das Licht der freilich schon sinkenden Sonne auf dem Gesicht des kindlichen Mädchens, das so geht und sich umschaut und zugleich sieht man den Schatten des Mannes darauf, der hinter ihm rascher kommt.

Dann ist der Mann schon vorübergegangen und das Gesicht des Kindes ist ganz hell.

Above. Passage from Kafka's first publication. Later entitled "Absent-minded Window-gazing" ("Zerstreutes Hinausschauen"), this is the second of eight prose pieces collectively titled *Meditation (Betrachtung)*. It appeared in the first issue of the journal *Hyperion,* published by Hans von Weber and edited by Franz Blei. (See Appendix.)

Below left. Franz Blei and his family. Kafka spent the "Night of the Comet" with them (the appearance of Halley's comet, May 17–18, 1910). The "discoverer" of the authors Robert Musil and Robert Walser, Blei was, along with Brod, the first active backer of Kafka. Kafka referred to him as "an admirable man. The passion and even more the variety of his talents have driven him into the densest thickets of literature, where, however, he can find neither release nor sustenance. Instead, with transformed energy, he liberates himself by founding journals."

Below right. Hans von Weber, publisher of *Hyperion.*

Opposite. The cover of volume I, number 1, of *Hyperion.*

HYPERION

EINE ZWEIMONATSSCHRIFT HERAUSGEGEBEN VON FRANZ BLEI & CARL STERNHEIM

MÜNCHEN 1908
HANS VON WEBER/VERLAG

Café Français (Felsche)
A. Goerger

In Leipzig on June 29, 1912, en route to Weimar, Kafka met the writers Walter Hasenclever and Kurt Pinthus, as well as the publishing partners Ernst Rowohlt and Kurt Wolff. Kafka notes in his diary: "Café Français. Rowohlt is quite serious about getting a book out of me." The result of the meeting was *Meditation*, his first book.

Above left. The Café Français in Leipzig. *Above right.* Ernst Rowohlt.

Below. Left to right, Walter Hasenclever, Franz Werfel, and Kurt Pinthus, Leipzig, 1912.

FRANZ KAFKA

———

BETRACHTUNG

The first book, *Meditation,* expanded now to eighteen short prose pieces, dedicated to Max Brod, and published by Ernst Rowohlt in Leipzig in November 1912.

Left. Three drawings by Emil Preetorius entitled "Sectio Siamesica" (the separation of Siamese twins), on the occasion of a "most interesting operation performed in Leipzig, about whose success, however, opinion is still divided." This was the split between Rowohlt (left) and Wolff (right) in November 1912. Rowohlt left the firm, which Wolff continued under his own name from the beginning of 1913.

Below left. Prospectus written by Franz Werfel for Kurt Wolff's new literary series "Der Jüngste Tag"—"The Newest Day." (See Appendix.) Initiated in 1913 for the publication of promising contemporary writing, it was designed and manufactured to sell at a low price. Three of Kafka's books appeared in this series: *The Stoker, The Metamorphosis,* and *The Judgment.*

Below right. The third printing (1917) of *The Stoker.* The celebrated uniform cover used for the series—a black cardboard binding with a pasted colored label—was necessitated by a shortage of printing materials during World War I.

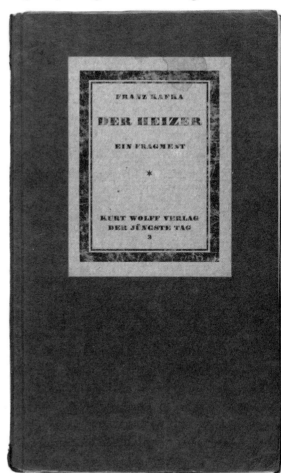

KURT WOLFF VERLAG
LEIPZIG
/Früher Ernst Rowohlt Verlag/

DER
JÜNGSTE TAG
NEUE DICHTUNGEN

Es sollen die stärksten Einheiten heutiger Dichtungen in einem neuen Unternehmen vereinigt werden, das nicht mehr an der Gebundenheit von Zeitschriften leiden wird. „Der jüngste Tag" soll mehr als ein Buch sein und weniger als eine Bücherei: er ist die Reihenfolge von Schöpfungen der jüngsten Dichter, hervorgebracht durch das gemeinsame Erlebnis unserer Zeit. In einzelnen zwanglosen Folgen werden von jetzt ab zum Preise von 80 Pfennigen für das geheftete, M 1.50 für das gebundene Buch, Werke jener Dichter erscheinen, deren Gestalt im Rahmen dieses neuen Geistes notwendig ist; sie sollen als ein kurzer, doch ungeheurer Abriß ihres Wollens und ihrer Idee zu billigstem Preise in weiteste Kreise dringen. „Der jüngste Tag" begrenzt sich mit keiner Clique, mit keiner Freund- noch Feindschaft, mit keiner Stadt und mit keinem Land. Er wird deshalb, getreu dem Spiegel seines Wortes, versuchen, alles notwendige zu sammeln, das ihm, aus der Stärke des Zeitlichen heraus, ewiges Dasein verspricht.

Wir bitten das Sortiment, unser Bemühen, junge, starke Dichter durchzusetzen, tatkräftig zu unterstützen.

DER JÜNGSTE TAG
NEUE
DICHTUNGEN

Franz
Kafka
Der
Heizer
Ein
Frag=
ment

LEIPZIG
KURT WOLFF VERLAG

Kafka's second book. Cover of the first edition of *The Stoker,* identical in content with the first chapter of *Der Verschollene (Amerika)* and thus designated "A Fragment." The imprint reads: "First published in May 1913 as the third volume in the literary series 'Der Jüngste Tag.'"

Von einer Vollversammlung Ihrer Verlagsautoren die besten Grüße

Sehr geehrter Herr Wolff! Glauben Sie Werfel nicht! Er kennt ja kein Wort von der Geschichte. Bis ich sie ins Reine werde haben schreiben lassen, schicke ich sie natürlich sehr gerne. Ihr ergebener

Otto Pick
Albert Ehrenstein
Carl Ehrenstein

F. Kafka

Left. A postcard from Berlin (March 24, 1913), signed by the literary figures Otto Pick, Albert and Carl Ehrenstein, Paul Zech, Franz Kafka, and (on the reverse) Elsa Lasker-Schüler, to their publisher, Kurt Wolff. Kafka's remark ("As soon as I have the whole thing transcribed, of course I'll send it to you") refers to *The Metamorphosis*; Franz Werfel had heard about the story and informed Wolff.

Below left. Kurt Wolff, the most important of Kafka's publishers.
Below right. Opening page of the first edition of *The Metamorphosis*. (See Appendix.)

I.

ALS Gregor Samsa eines Morgens aus unruhigen Träumen erwachte, fand er sich in seinem Bett zu einem ungeheueren Ungeziefer verwandelt. Er lag auf seinem panzerartig harten Rücken und sah, wenn er den Kopf ein wenig hob, seinen gewölbten, braunen, von bogenförmigen Versteifungen geteilten Bauch, auf dessen Höhe sich die Bettdecke, zum gänzlichen Niedergleiten bereit, kaum noch erhalten konnte. Seine vielen, im Vergleich zu seinem sonstigen Umfang kläglich dünnen Beine flimmerten ihm hilflos vor den Augen.

»Was ist mit mir geschehen?«, dachte er. Es war kein Traum. Sein Zimmer, ein richtiges, nur etwas zu kleines Menschenzimmer, lag ruhig zwischen den vier wohlbekannten Wänden. Über dem Tisch, auf dem eine auseinandergepackte Musterkollektion von Tuchwaren ausgebreitet war — Samsa war Reisender —, hing das Bild, das er vor kurzem aus einer illustrierten Zeitschrift ausgeschnitten und in einem hübschen, vergoldeten Rahmen untergebracht hatte. Es stellte eine Dame dar, die, mit einem Pelzhut und einer Pelzboa versehen, aufrecht dasaß und einen schweren Pelzmuff, in dem ihr ganzer Unterarm verschwunden war, dem Beschauer entgegenhob.

Gregors Blick richtete sich dann zum Fenster, und das trübe Wetter — man hörte Regentropfen auf das Fensterblech aufschlagen — machte ihn ganz melancholisch. »Wie wäre es, wenn ich noch ein wenig weiter-

3

FRANZ KAFKA

DIE VERWANDLUNG

DER JÜNGSTE TAG ★ 22/23

KURT WOLFF VERLAG · LEIPZIG

1916

Kafka's third book, *The Metamorphosis,* published in November 1915 as a two-number volume (22/23) in the "Newest Day" series. The cover illustration is a lithograph by Ottomar Starke. When Kafka learned that Starke was to do an illustration, he wrote: "The insect itself must not be illustrated by a drawing. It cannot be shown at all, not even from a distance."

DAS URTEIL

EINE GESCHICHTE
VON
FRANZ KAFKA

LEIPZIG

KURT WOLFF VERLAG

1 9 1 6

Above left. A notice of the bestowing of the Fontane Prize (a coveted German literary award) on the playwright Carl Sternheim; the article mentions Sternheim's passing the award money on to Kafka as a token of his esteem. *Prager Tagblatt,* December 6, 1915. (See Appendix.)

Above. Georg Heinrich Meyer, director of Kurt Wolff's publishing house after 1914. A "business geniüs," he ran the firm almost single-handed during the first years of the war. In October 1915 he informed Kafka that *The Metamorphosis* (the manuscript of which had been in house for a long time) had to be set in type instantly; he had been told "confidentially," in connection with the Fontane Prize, that "general attention will be shifted in your direction." As a result of all this activity, a separate book edition of *Das Urteil* ("The Judgment," together with other stories) appeared in October 1916, to Kafka's great satisfaction.

Left. Title page of the first edition of *The Judgment* in the "Newest Day" series.

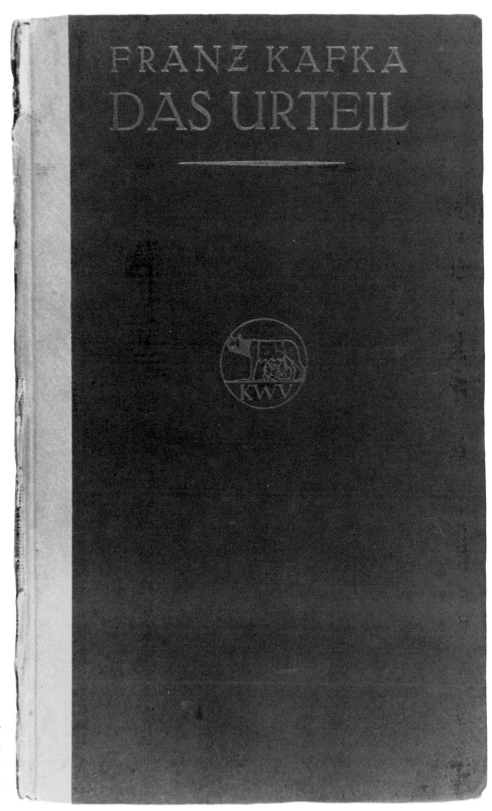

FRANZ KAFKA
DAS URTEIL

Kafka's fourth book, *The Judgment,* first printed in October 1916 as volume 34 of the "Newest Day" series. Shown here is the bibliophile edition with parchment spine.

Drawings by Kafka.

According to Max Brod, Kafka was already drawing sketches as a university student, doodling in the margins of his "scripts" (the printed notes taken from the professors' lectures and used in cramming for examinations). Most of the sketches on these two pages (made available to the author by Max Brod in 1956) probably date from Kafka's university days, with the exception of the six directly to the left, which were probably made somewhat later.

Opposite, upper left. This drawing was clearly made when Kafka was taking riding lessons and going to the horse races in Kuchelbad near Prague. To its right is a drawing captioned in Kafka's hand "Petitioner and Distinguished Patron." The sketch below these two is probably connected with the scene of the litter bearers in the early story "Description of a Struggle."

In Kafka's later manuscripts, in his diaries, in the octavo notebooks, and on postcards one often comes across little caricatures or illustrative sketches. In 1921 Gustav Janouch found him doodling at his desk in the insurance company. Kafka told him it was "an old and deeply ingrained addiction."

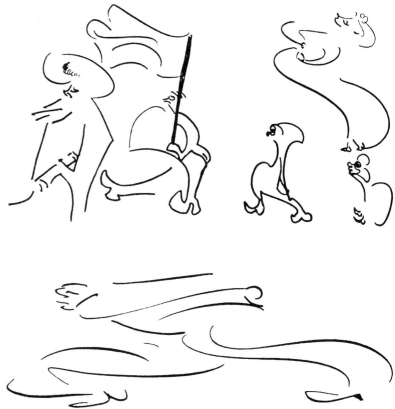

Passport photograph, 1915–1916.

To Live or to Write, 1913–1917

The weeks of extraordinary literary productivity following the September night in 1912 when Kafka wrote "The Judgment" were accompanied by a "flood of letters" to Felice Bauer in Berlin, where she was working for a dictaphone or "parlograph" company. In the first three months he wrote her more than one hundred letters; in the next eight months, more than two hundred. In addition, he twice visited her in Berlin during the first half of 1913. The alarming magnitude of this correspondence was bound, of course, increasingly to displace his literary production. Kafka saw it as a choice between "living" and "writing," which he first tried to forestall by working during the afternoons as a gardener and at the Pomological Institute in Troja. Soon after he had proposed to Felice in June, their contact abruptly broke off. Kafka felt himself "chained by invisible chains to an invisible literature."

In September 1913 he attended a convention in Vienna devoted to industrial accident prevention, went from there "infinitely unhappy" to Venice, and then by way of Verona and Desenzano to Riva on Lake Garda. Here he stayed at a sanatorium, met "the Swiss girl," and had a love affair about which he revealed as little as he had about the earlier affair in Zuckmantel.

Kafka's literary productivity, however, did not reassert itself as expected, nor were renewed contacts with Felice (arranged by her friend Grete Bloch and by Ernst Weiss) more than sporadic: thirteen letters and two more visits with her in Berlin. He wrote in his diary March 9, 1914:

I couldn't marry then; everything in me revolted against it, much as I always loved F. It was chiefly concern over my literary work that prevented me, for I thought marriage would jeopardize it. I may have been right, but in any case it is destroyed by my present bachelor's life. I have written nothing for a year, nor shall I be able to write anything in the future; in my head there is and remains the one single thought, and I am devoured by it.

Then suddenly, after a third trip to Berlin, the two were "unofficially" engaged to be married. The official engagement, which took place in Berlin at Whitsuntide with Kafka's parents in attendance, was inauspicious from the start. He refers to himself in the diaries as being "tied up like a criminal." Only six weeks later "the courtroom drama at the hotel" took place in Berlin, in the presence of Bloch and Weiss, with Bloch as "judge." The engagement was broken. Kafka then left with Weiss and Weiss's friend Rahel Sanzara for the Danish sea resort of Marielyst on the Baltic coast, where they stayed for two weeks.

At the outbreak of World War I Kafka was back in Prague, "more determined than ever." His diary entry for August 15, 1914, says: "I have been writing these past few days, may it continue. Today I am not so completely protected by and enclosed in my work as I was two years ago, nevertheless have the feeling that my monotonous, empty, mad bachelor's life has some justification. I can once more carry on a conversation with myself, and don't stare so into complete emptiness. Only in this way is there any possibility of improvement for me."

Since he was "physically unfit for military service,"

he was not called up. His two brothers-in-law, on the other hand, were drafted, and their wives returned to the elder Kafkas' home in the Oppelt House, obliging Kafka to look for an apartment of his own. This proved difficult; at first he moved into his sister Valli's place on the Bilekgasse, then into Elli's on the Nerudagasse, then back to the Bilekgasse for a month, until he finally found an apartment of his own on the Lange Gasse in March 1915. Despite these complications, he managed during these months to write long sections of *The Trial* (*Der Prozess*), the "final" chapter of *Der Verschollene* (*Amerika*), and "In the Penal Colony" ("In der Strafkolonie"). Then once more the creative impulse vanished.

In January 1915, Kafka and Felice had met again in the Austro-German border town of Tetschen-Bodenbach. Kafka's diary is revealing:

We have found each other quite unchanged. . . . Each of us silently says to himself that the other is immovable and merciless. I yield not a particle of my demand for a fantastic life arranged solely in the interest of my work; she, indifferent to every mute request, wants the average: a comfortable home, an interest on my part in the factory, good food, bed at eleven, central heating; sets my watch—which for the past three months has been an hour and a half fast—right to the minute. And she is right in the end and would continue to be right in the end; she is right when she corrects the bad German I used to the waiter, and I can put nothing right when she speaks of the "personal touch" (it cannot be said any way but gratingly) in the furnishings she intends to have in her home. . . .

We haven't yet had a single good moment together during which I could have breathed freely. With F. I never experienced (except in letters) that sweetness one experiences in a relationship with a woman one loves, such as I had in Zuckmantel and Riva—only unlimited admiration, humility, sympathy, despair and self-contempt.

The situation was not much improved during a spring trip they took together to the mountainous region known as Bohemian Switzerland; Kafka spent his summer vacation alone at the sanatorium in Rumburg. The turning point did not come until the summer of 1916, when the two vacationed together in Marienbad: "Things are different now and good. In brief, we are contracted to be married right after the war is over."

Even a rather unsuccessful reading of "In the Penal Colony" in Munich did not demoralize him; Kafka returned home "with renewed courage." His creative drive had reasserted itself and was further encouraged from November 1916 by the productive atmosphere of a little private house Ottla had rented on the Alchimistengasse where he could work at night undisturbed. He described this refuge in a letter to Felice:

To sum up its advantages: the lovely way up to it, the quiet there—from my sole neighbor I am separated by only a very thin wall—but the neighbor is quiet enough, and generally stays there until midnight; and then the benefit of the walk home: I have to make up my mind to stop. I then have the walk that cools my head. And the life there: it is something special to have one's own house, to shut in the face of the world the door not of your room, not of your flat, but of your own house; to step out through the door of your lodgings straight into the snow of a quiet alley.

The same productive solitude was later provided by new lodgings in the Schönborn Palais, into which Kafka moved in March 1917. In these two places he wrote nearly all the stories comprised in the *Country Doctor* collection, in addition to many shorter prose pieces.

In August, several weeks after their second official engagement and a short trip with Felice to Budapest, the "illness which had been coaxed into revealing itself after [five years of] headaches and sleeplessness" broke out—that "coughing up of blood" that Kafka calls "almost a relief."

For the eventuality that in the near future I may die or become wholly unfit to live—the probability of it is great, since in the last two nights I have coughed a good deal of blood—let me say that I myself have torn myself to shreds. If my father in earlier days was in the habit of uttering wild but empty threats, saying: I'll tear you apart like a fish—in fact, he did not so much as lay a finger on me—now the threat is being fulfilled independently of him. The world—F is its representative—and my ego are tearing my body apart in a conflict that there is no resolving.

TO LIVE
OR TO WRITE

Left. The Anhalt Station in Berlin, where the trains from Prague arrived. The building at far right is the Hotel Askanischer Hof (see page 164), where Kafka customarily stayed, as was the case in March 1915, when he first visited his fiancée-to-be, Felice Bauer ("the Berlin girl").

Left center. A Berlin taxi in 1912.

Below left. The Immanuelkirchstrasse, Berlin. The Bauer family lived in the right-hand corner building until April 1913.

Below. Felice Bauer in 1914. Her signature is beneath the photograph.

Above. The Pomological Institute in Troja near Prague, beyond the Baumgarten, or Royal Forest Park, on the Moldau. In 1913 and occasionally thereafter, Kafka worked here as a gardener, a favorite avocation.

Right. In the Baumgarten.

Below. An old photograph of a stretch of meadows along the banks of the Moldau in winter, showing the ferry across to Troja; one of Kafka's cherished spots. "On the left one sees the river and beyond it sloping land, sparsely covered with trees. Just opposite me, a solitary hill with an old house nestled gently against the landscape, a place that has seemed mysterious to me ever since my childhood; and round about it peaceful, undulating land."

Internationaler Kongreß für Rettungswesen.
Vom Geheimen Rat Dr. Moritz Grafen Vetter von der Lilie.
Präsident des Kongresses.

Wien, 6. September.

Unter dem Protektorat des Erzherzogs Leopold Salvator findet in den Tagen vom 9. bis 13. d. der zweite internationale Kongreß für Rettungswesen und Unfallverhütung in Wien statt. Das Parlament wird die Tore öffnen, um diesen Kongreß willkommen zu heißen, und das Bureau der Wiener Freiwilligen Rettungsgesellschaft hat alle komplizierten Vorarbeiten in mustergültiger Weise geleistet. Wien wird in der nächsten Zeit mehrere wissenschaftliche Vereinigungen begrüßen — die erste, die Rettungswesen und Unfallverhütung zu Verhandlungsgegenständen hat, verdient das wärmste Interesse jedes Arztes, der Behörden, jedes Samariters und Menschenfreundes. Die Einbeziehung der Unfallverhütung sei besonders hervorgehoben.

Der Unterricht in der ersten Hilfe wird ein wichtiges Thema der Beratungen bilden. Wie von der Qualität des ersten Verbandes auf dem Schlachtfelde das Schicksal des Verwundeten abhängt, so ist die erste Hilfe bei den alltäglichen Unglücksfällen von größter Bedeutung für die Prognose. Für die weite Oeffentlichkeit ist die Kenntnis der richtigen Prinzipien, nach welchen die erste Hilfe zu leisten ist, sehr wichtig, die Popularisierung dieser Kenntnis von nicht zu unterschätzender Bedeutung für jedermann. Um den Kongreß schlingt sich ein Band von gesellschaftlichen Veranstaltungen, die heute nicht besprochen werden sollen.

Venezia.   Canal grande preso dall' Accademia e palazzo Franchetti.

Above left: An article in the *Neue Freie Presse* (New Free Press), Vienna, on an "International Congress for Rescue Services and Accident Prevention" held September 9–13, 1913, which Kafka attended with his superiors Eugen Pfohl and Robert Marschner, director of the Workers Accident Insurance Company.

Above.   Amusement-park photograph from the Prater in Vienna. Left to right: Kafka, Albert Ehrenstein, Otto Pick, and Lise Kaznelson. These three were in Vienna for the Eleventh Zionist Congress when Kafka was there.
Below.   The harbor at Trieste. Following the meetings, Kafka took time off for a vacation trip alone, from Vienna by train to Trieste and from there by ship to Venice.

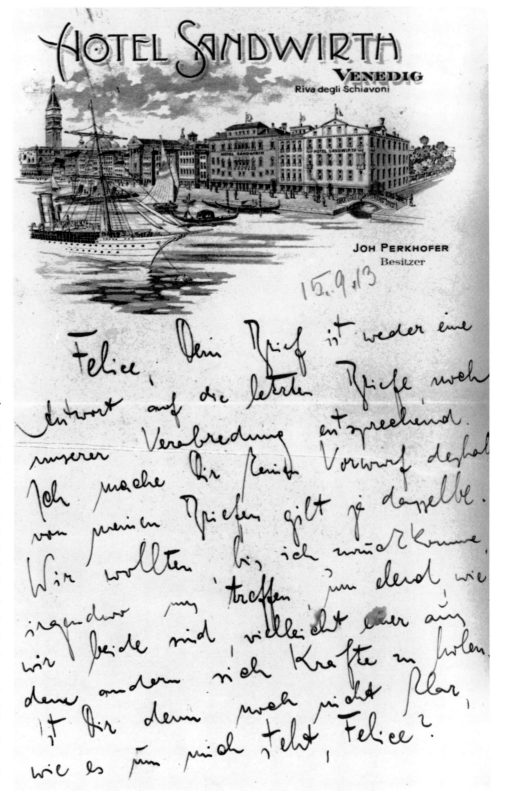

Letter from Kafka to Felice, written from Venice September 15, 1913, the last of more than two hundred letters and postcards he had been sending her since the beginning of the year. "Felice, your letter is neither an answer to my earlier ones nor is it written in the spirit of our agreement. I am not reproaching you for that, for the same can be said for my letters. We had planned to meet somewhere on my return, in order, wretched as we both are, to try to find some source of strength in one another. Are you still not aware of how matters stand with me, Felice?..." Kafka remained in Venice for several days, "infinitely unhappy" and "sad to the point of overflowing."

Left. A "Kaiserpanorama" photograph of the interior of Saint Anastasia in Verona, where Kafka stopped on his way to Desenzano and Riva. Years later he recalled "the life-size marble dwarf with the happy expression on his face, supporting a holy-water font" (far right).

Below. Steamer plying between Desenzano and Riva.

Bottom. Desenzano on Lake Garda. Most of the townspeople assembled to welcome Dr. Kafka, vice-secretary of the insurance company, on September 21, 1913. But he lay on the grass at the edge of the lake, "empty and aimless, even in the awareness of my misery. If only I were on my way to a deserted island instead of the sanatorium."

Right. Dr. von Hartungen's Sanatorium and Hydrotherapy Institute in Riva: the main building; the dining hall; and the reclining loggia on the lake.

Below: The harbor of Riva. In September–October 1913 Kafka spent three weeks at the sanatorium nearby, "greedy for solitude," at least in the beginning. Presently, he fell in love with "the Swiss girl," an eighteen-year-old who was also a guest there. This was Kafka's second affair (the first was at Zuckmantel) that he described as filled with "the sweetness one experiences in a relationship with a woman one loves." Riva also provided him with the locale for his story "The Hunter Gracchus" (*gracchus* = jackdaw = *kavka*).

Left. The Altstädter Ring in Prague with the Niklas-kirche (the Russian Orthodox Church) and the Oppelt House (right; the Kafkas moved into the top-floor apartment in November 1913).

Below. View from the Altstädter Ring down the Niklasstrasse to the Moldau. The City Hall at left, the Oppelt House at right.

Bottom. Two recent photographs taken from Kafka's room, looking out on the Niklasstrasse; the Niklas-kirche at left, apartment buildings at right. The church was known at the time as "the Russian church." Kafka writes: "Directly opposite my window I have the great dome of the Russian church with its two towers."

Right. The parents' mantel clock, one of the very few family objects that have survived.

Below right. Kafka with Ottla, his favorite sister, standing in front of the Oppelt House to the left of the main entrance, around 1914. Kafka's bandaged left thumb is probably the one about which he says in a letter that he is treating it in "the natural-health way, whereby it is healing ten times more slowly, to be sure, but a hundred times more beautifully, without inflammation, without swelling, a veritable delight to the eye."

Below. A recent photograph of the main entrance of the Oppelt House.

171

Wilmersdorfer Strasse, Ecke Mommsen-Strasse — Charlottenburg

Above. Felice and Franz's engagement announcement in the *Berliner Tageblatt,* April 21, 1914.

Left. View from the Bauers' apartment, Wilmersdorferstrasse 73, Berlin-Charlottenburg. Kafka reminded Felice's mother of the time "when with a friendly wave from your balcony you saw me off on my last walk down the Mommsenstrasse."

Center left. The Deutsche Werkstätten (German Workshop Studios) in Hellerau near Dresden, which Kafka visited in June 1914. Kafka esteemed the products of this pioneering workshop for modern furniture as "the best and simplest," whereas Felice preferred "the heavy furniture which other families of your and also of my class had."

Below left. A suite of living-room furniture made by the Deutsche Werkstätten.

Below. Grete Bloch, a friend of Felice Bauer.

Above. Letterhead of the Hotel Askanischer Hof, where Kafka customarily stayed when he was in Berlin. It was here on July 12, 1914, in the presence of Grete Bloch and Ernst Weiss, that "the courtroom drama in the hotel" took place; the phrase from Kafka's diary refers to the dissolution of his engagement to Felice.

Right. The writer Ernst Weiss (Kafka's friend) and his companion, the actress Rachel Sanzara. Kafka went with these two to Marielyst, a Danish seaside resort on the Baltic, after the breaking off of his engagement to Felice.

Below. Marielyst. A postcard to Ottla, July 21, 1914, with the laconic remark "Things are going relatively well with me."

173

Left. Kafka, about 1917.

Below left. Austrian army recruits at the outbreak of World War I, August 1914. During this same month Kafka began work on *The Trial;* two months later he wrote "In the Penal Colony." His diary for August 6, 1914, reads: "The artillery troops marching along the Graben. Flowers, shouts of 'Heil' and 'Nazdar.' . . .

"I feel nothing but pettiness within myself, no capacity for anything decisive, envy and hatred of the warriors for whom, with a passion, I wish everything bad.

"Patriotic parades. A speech by the lord mayor. All disappear, then reappear and shout in German, 'Long live our beloved Monarch. Hurrah!' I stand there and watch, with my wicked stare."

Below. The first page of the 1919 edition of *In the Penal Colony.* (See Appendix.)

„Es ist ein eigentümlicher Apparat," sagte der Offizier zu dem Forschungsreisenden und überblickte mit einem gewissermassen bewundernden Blick den ihm doch wohlbekannten Apparat. Der Reisende schien nur aus Höflichkeit der Einladung des Kommandanten gefolgt zu sein, der ihn aufgefordert hatte, der Exekution eines Soldaten beizuwohnen, der wegen Ungehorsam und Beleidigung des Vorgesetzten verurteilt worden war. Das Interesse für diese Exekution war wohl auch in der Strafkolonie nicht sehr gross. Wenigstens war hier in dem tiefen, sandigen, von kahlen Abhängen ringsum abgeschlossenen kleinen Tal ausser dem Offizier und dem Reisenden nur der Verurteilte, ein stumpfsinniger, breitmäuliger Mensch mit verwahrlostem Haar und Gesicht und ein Soldat zu-

5

Above. Some lines from the manuscript of *The Trial*. (See Appendix.)
Right. Prague, Bilekgasse 10. Kafka lived in his sister Valli's apartment here during the first weeks of the war and began writing *The Trial*.
Below. Elli's apartment house, Prague-Weinberge, Nerudagasse 48 (today Polská Ulice). From September 1914 to January 1915 further chapters of *The Trial* and the story "In the Penal Colony" were written here.

Above left. The church of Saint Barbara in Kuttenberg, where Kafka and Brod spent a brief vacation toward the end of 1914. *Right.* Edmundsklamm (Edmund's Gorge) in "Bohemian Switzerland," visited on an excursion with Felice and Grete Bloch. *Below.* Tetschen-Bodenbach. In January 1915 Kafka and Felice met here, for the first time after their engagement was broken. *Below left.* The "House of the Golden Pike," Lange Gasse 18, Prague. In March 1915, Kafka moved into a corner room on the top floor of this pension. It was the first time he had ever had a place of his own. He was thirty-one years old.

In July 1915 Kafka spent two weeks at the Frankenstein Sanatorium near Rumburg in northern Bohemia. In May 1917 this sanatorium became a "Neurological Health Center for Veterans and Civilians" and was patronized by an organization that Kafka supported. He returned to Rumburg frequently thereafter to work on behalf of the center.

Above. The marketplace in Rumburg, on a postcard to Felice, July 1915.

Near right. Photograph of the sanatorium, taken in the 1930s.

Far right and below. Views of the sanatorium today.

Left. The Kreuzbrunnen Colonnade in Marienbad.

Left center. The hotel Castle Balmoral and Osborne, where Kafka and Felice stayed in July 1916.

Lower left. View of the spa at Franzensbad.

Below. Kafka's mother and Valli in Franzensbad, 1917. *Bottom.* Photograph of the family at Franzensbad: Valli, mother, father with grandson Felix, and Elli on the far right.

Other than Prague, Munich was the only place where Kafka ever gave a public reading from his works. He read "In the Penal Colony" there in November 1916. Felice came from Berlin for the reading. The event was a failure; of the barely fifty people who came, several left before it was over. The press was likewise negative: "repulsive material"; "anything but riveting"; the author was "a voluptuary of horror."

Above. Cover of the first edition of *In the Penal Colony,* published by Kurt Wolff in 1919.

Above right. Sketch by Friedrich Feigl of Kafka reading "The Bucket Rider" ("Der Kübelreiter") at a private gathering in Prague. This is the single artistic representation of Kafka made during his life.

Right. The Hotel Bayerischer Hof, Munich, where Felice and Kafka stayed in November 1916.

Above. The Belvedere in the Chotek Park, a frequent goal of the walks Kafka took with his sister Ottla (*below*).

Left. The Alchimistengasse on the Hradschin. House number 22, the dark façade in left foreground, was rented by Ottla in November 1916 and made available to her brother. Here he wrote many of the stories later incorporated in the *Country Doctor* collection.

Above. A page from one of the "octavo notebooks" Kafka used at this period. (See Appendix.)

Right. The Nerudagasse as it ascends to the Hradschin.

Below. Ancient flight of steps leading up to the Hradschin. "Beautiful—the walk back home around midnight, down the old castle steps to the city."

Above left.   The Schönborn Palais, at Marktgasse 15, below the Hradschin. In March 1917 Kafka moved from the Lange Gasse into this building. His room was on the third floor, with a view of the street. Here in August 1917 Kafka suffered the hemorrhage that signaled the onset of his tuberculosis.

Above right.   The Cathedral of Saint Vitus on the Hradschin.

Below.   The Graben in Vienna. The Emperor Franz Josef Bridge in Budapest. Kafka's and Felice's last trip together took them from Prague (where they became engaged for the second time) to Vienna and then on to Budapest.

Felice and Kafka in Budapest, early July 1917.

Passport photograph,
1920.

The Final Years, 1917–1924

The onset of Kafka's tuberculosis in the summer of 1917 ended, for the time being, all "attempts at marriage" and liberated him from his job at the insurance company.

What happened was that the brain could no longer endure the burden of worry and suffering heaped upon it. It said: "I give up; but should there be someone still interested in the maintenance of the whole, then he must relieve me of some of my burden and things will still go on for a while." Then the lung spoke up, though it probably hadn't much to lose anyhow. These discussions between brain and lung which went on without my knowledge may have been terrible.

But the relief was never more than temporary; after allowing periods for recuperation, Kafka's firm in the next five years repeatedly demanded his "return to duty."

Beginning in September 1917, Kafka lived for nearly eight months in Zürau in northwestern Bohemia, a tiny village in the midst of hop fields where Ottla was working on a "small estate," having been encouraged by her brother to pursue her interest in agricultural studies and farming. This was for Kafka, the city dweller, his first extended stay in a rural setting. He accomplished no major literary work in Zürau, but certain initial inspirations for *The Castle (Das Schloss)* probably date from this time. He also continued the Hebrew studies begun in Prague as preparation for a trip to Palestine, a plan he nurtured to the end of his life.

After a half-year's work at the office, he was granted another leave. Beginning in November 1918, he lived for four months in a boarding house in Liboch on the Elbe, a place he had known from many summer trips. At the Pension Stüdl he met Minze Eisner (with whom he later carried on a long correspondence about her career plans) and, more important, Julie Wohryzek, daughter of a shoemaker and synagogue custodian in Prague, to whom he soon became engaged. This union was vigorously opposed by his father, a reaction that inspired Kafka's bitter *Letter to His Father,* written during a subsequent one-month stay at the same *pension* in November 1919.

You said to me something like this: "She probably put on a fancy blouse, something these Prague Jewesses are good at, and right away, of course, you decided to marry her. And that as fast as possible, in a week, tomorrow, today. I can't understand you: after all, you're a grown man, you live in the city, and you don't know what to do but marry the next best girl. Isn't there anything else you can do? If you're frightened, I'll go with you." . . . *You put it in more detail and more plainly.* . . .

You have hardly ever humiliated me more deeply with words and shown me your contempt more clearly.

The engagement collapsed.

Not until April 1920 did Kafka's company approve another medical leave; this time, Kafka went to Merano for three months. From there, he wrote his first letters to Milena Jesenská, his Czech translator, who lived in Vienna. A new love affair began in this correspondence and prompted Kafka to visit Milena in Vienna for several days on his roundabout return trip from Merano to Prague. In mid-August the two met once more in Gmünd, an Austrian border town. Then this attempt at an enduring relationship also came to nothing, like all the others before it. Too much stood in the way: Milena was married, a Christian, and a Czech; Kafka hardly felt up to facing the predictable opposition from his family and society. Nevertheless, their exceptionally intimate and trusting relationship continued for a long time. More than a year later, in October 1921, Kafka entrusted the safekeeping of all his diaries to Milena.

The end of the love affair was followed in the fall of 1920 by a brief but intense rebirth of literary production after a fallow period of nearly three years. Kafka wrote many parables during this time, among them "Poseidon," "At Night," and "On the Problem of Our Laws." But by December the source of inspiration was once again dry. Kafka went to the High Tatra on the mountainous Polish border, where he remained for eight months, living with other tubercular patients for the first time. A close friendship with one of them, Robert Klopstock, lasted to the end of Kafka's life.

In the late summer of 1921 the insurance company again insisted on Kafka's return to work. After another brief leave spent at Spindelmühle, he was finally relieved of all duties in June of 1922, when he was granted retirement on the grounds of poor health. The previous February at Spindelmühle he had begun work on *The Castle;* he continued it in Prague and then at Ottla's summer place in Planá on the Luschnitz. During the same period he wrote "Investigations of a Dog" ("Forschungen eines Hundes"), "First Sorrow" ("Erstes Leid"), and "A Hunger Artist" ("Ein Hungerkünstler"). In September, Kafka wrote Brod from Planá that he had "had to abandon the 'castle story,' apparently forever."

It was not until a full year later, after a long sojourn in Prague, that Kafka began to write once again. On a summer vacation trip with his sister Elli to Müritz on the Baltic coast, he had met Dora Diamant at the resort colony of the Berlin Jewish People's Home; in September he and Dora moved together into an apartment in Berlin. Kafka had finally realized his dream of leaving Prague.

The days are so short, pass for me even faster than in Prague, and happily much less noticeably. Of course it is a pity that they pass so swiftly, but that is the way time is; once you've taken your hand off its wheel it starts to spin and you no longer see a place for your hand to check it. I scarcely go beyond the immediate vicinity of the apartment, but this neighborhood is wonderful; my street is about the last half-urban one. Beyond it the countryside breaks up into gardens and villas, old, lush gardens. On warm evenings there is a strong fragrance, stronger almost than anything I have encountered elsewhere. Then in addition there are the great botanical gardens, a fifteen-minute walk from where I am, and the woods, where I have not yet been, are less than half an hour. So the setting for this little emigrant is beautiful.

Here, in the middle of the appalling "winter of inflation," 1923–1924, he wrote "A Little Woman" ("Eine kleine Frau"), "The Burrow" ("Der Bau"), and many other stories, which are now lost. He even managed to conclude a contract with a new publisher for his next book, *A Hunger Artist*; it was to appear only after his death.

In mid-March, Max Brod brought his mortally ill friend back to Prague. In April, Dora Diamant and Robert Klopstock accompanied Kafka to a sanatorium in Kierling near Vienna. He died there on June 3, 1924.

A pupil mocks his teacher who speaks of nothing but death: "You talk about death all the time but still you don't die." "And I'll die all the same, I'm just singing my last song. One man's song is longer, another's shorter. The difference, however, can never be more than a few words."

This is true, and it's unjust to smile about the hero who lies mortally wounded on the stage and sings an aria. We lie on the ground and sing for years.

THE FINAL
YEARS

Der Vizesekretär Dr. F r a n z
K a f k a ist an einem ärztlich
konstatierten Lungenspitzenkatarrh
erkrankt und seit 11.September l.J.
aus dem büro weggeblieben.

Prag, 14/9 1917.

Above.   Zürau. Kafka and his sister Ottla.
Left.   Insurance company notes regarding Kafka's
"absence" for medical reasons. (See Appendix.)
Below.   Ottla with Cousin Irma in Zürau.

Top. General view of the village of Zürau, district of Podersam, in a recent photograph. *Above left.* The market-place in Zürau. Behind the tree to the right of the church is the house (since demolished) where Kafka lived for nearly eight months. Next door, the house "with the only piano in northwestern Bohemia," as Kafka laments. *Above right.* View from the abandoned site of the house in a recent photograph. *Below.* Zürau in an old photograph.

HERMANN KAFKA
PRAG I.,
ALTSTADTERRING No. 16
Palais Kinsky.

GALANTERIEWAREN EN GROS.

Sachverständiger des k. k. Landes- als Strafgerichtes.

Postsparkassen-Konto No. 2.131.
TELEFON No. 141.

PRAG, den 23/I 1918

Meine lieben Kinder!

Ich habe Euch vorigen geschrieben und hoffe, dass Ihr meinen Brief erhalten habt. Schreibt uns, wie es Euch geht, insbesondere ob Ihr gesund seid. Später sende ich Euch Briefe. Gabrielle und Cousine und hofft, dass Euch alles gut schmecken wird.

Ich grüsse und küsse Euch recht und bleibe Eure treue Mutter

Julie

Letter to Kafka and his sister Ottla in Zürau from their mother, January 23, 1918. (See Appendix.)

190

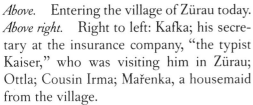

Above. Entering the village of Zürau today.

Above right. Right to left: Kafka; his secretary at the insurance company, "the typist Kaiser," who was visiting him in Zürau; Ottla; Cousin Irma; Mařenka, a housemaid from the village.

Right. The same group without Kafka (who evidently took this photograph) but with Fräulein Kaiser's fiancé.

Below. Franz and Anna Lüftner, owners of a neighboring farm, from the photograph medallion on their gravestone. Kafka visited them often.

Below right. The road to Oberklee, Kafka's favorite walk in the area.

Above. The Pension Stüdl in Schelesen near Liboch, where Kafka stayed in the winter of 1918–1919 with his second fiancée, Julie Wohryzek, and in November 1919, when he wrote the *Letter to His Father.* The second-floor balcony behind the tree belonged to his room. *Below.* The castle in Liboch on the Elbe.

Above. View of the Pension Stüdl from the sandstone cliff above the house. *Below.* View taken in the opposite direction from the photograph above. The colossal monster heads were carved into the rock by the sculptor Lévy in the early nineteenth century.

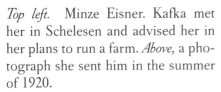

Top left. Minze Eisner. Kafka met her in Schelesen and advised her in her plans to run a farm. *Above,* a photograph she sent him in the summer of 1920.

Above right. A path near Schelesen.

Near right. The boardinghouse at Smečka 6, Prague-Weinberge, where Julie Wohryzek lived. There is no known photograph of Julie.

Far right. Liboch, the path to the church.

Above. Merano in the Italian province of Alto Adige. The Gilf Promenade as seen from Zeno Castle.

Left. The Pension Ottoburg in Merano-Untermais, where Kafka stayed from April into June 1920. Here he began his correspondence with the Czech translator of *The Stoker,* Milena Jesenská, with whom he subsequently became involved.

Below left. Garden façade of the Pension Ottoburg.

Below. First lines of one of Kafka's letters to Milena, 1922. (See Appendix.)

Above. Photographs of Milena (second from left, with friend Staša Jilovská). *Right.* Ernst Pollak, Milena's husband, and his favorite café in Vienna, the Herrenhof (recent photo). *Below.* Lerchenfeldstrasse 113, Vienna, where Milena lived (third floor). *Below right.* Gmünd near Vienna, on a postcard to Ottla. Kafka and Milena met here in August 1920.

Gmünd

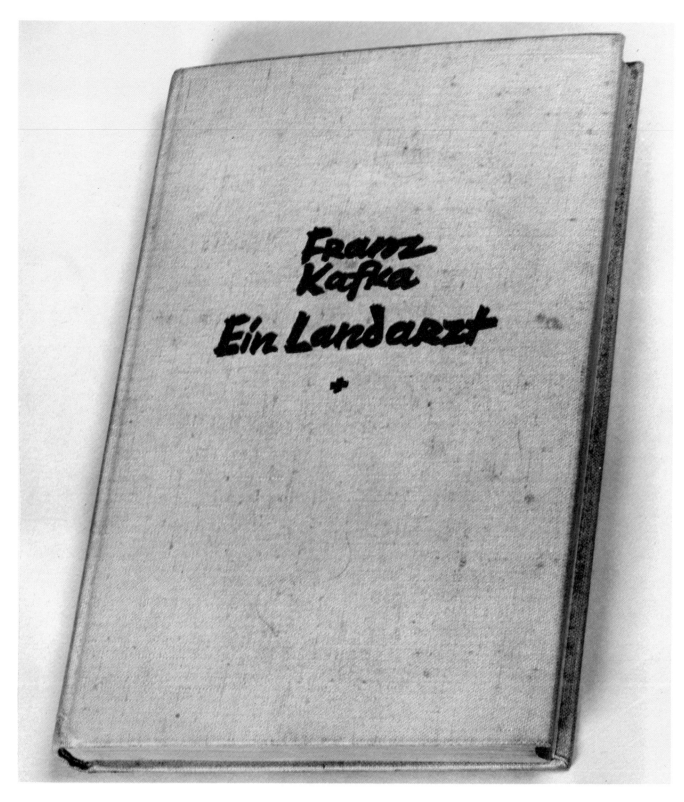

Linen-bound edition of the short-story collection *A Country Doctor,* published by Kurt Wolff in late 1920.

Above. Matlárháza, Kafka's sanatorium in Matliary in the High Tatra from December 1920 to August 1921. The closer of the two second-floor balconies belonged to Kafka's room.

Right. Postcard to Ottla from Matliary, August 8, 1921. *Below.* Sanatorium guests: first row, left to right, Robert Klopstock, the dentist Glauber, Kafka; above them, Irene Bugsch, Frau Galgon, unidentified woman, Margarete Bugsch; third row, right, Ilene Roth. Picture at the right shows the same group.

Above. View of Spindelmühle, a resort in German Silesia, with the Ziegenrücken (Goat's Back) in the distance. Kafka spent several weeks here in January and February 1922 and, after a long pause in his work, began to write again. The first chapters of *The Castle* were written here.

Left. A "horned sled" of the type Kafka often used at Spindelmühle.

Below. Saint Peter's Valley at Spindelmühle; to its right, the bridge over the Elbe at the entrance to the village.

Right. Josef David and Ottla. They were married in 1920. For their vacation in the summer of 1922 they rented a two-room apartment for themselves and their one-year-old daughter in Planá on the Luschnitz in southern Bohemia. At the end of June, Kafka joined them. During the next four months he wrote the last nine chapters of *The Castle* here.

Below. The vacation house in Planá. The two top-floor windows belonged to Kafka's room.

Planá on the Luschnitz.

Above. The train station (on the Prague–Vienna line).

Above left. The village center.

Left. The Luschnitz River. The two pictures below on the left show views of what was Kafka's daily "walk in the woods."

Below. Two views of the sawmill nearby. In his letters Kafka complains about the racket it made. The mill is still in operation.

Opposite. The first page of the fifth manuscript notebook of *The Castle.* (See Appendix.)

und wir einigten uns. Es ist auch schon alles ausgeführt. Ich bin Zimmer-
Kellnerin in Herrenhof und Frieda ist wieder im Ausschank. Es ist für Frieda
besser. Es lag für sie keine Vernunft darin Deine Frau zu werden. Auch
hast Du das Opfer, das sie Dir bringen wollte nicht zu würdigen ver-
standen. Nun hat aber der Gute noch immer manchmal Zweifel,
ob Dir nicht Unrecht geschehn ist ob Du vielleicht doch nicht bei
den Barnabas'schen warst. Trotzdem natürlich gar kein Zweifel daran
sein konnte wo Du warst, bin ich doch noch gegangen ein für allemal
festzustellen; denn nach all den
Aufregungen verdient es Frieda endlich einmal ruhig zu schlafen
ich allerdings auch. Ich bin also gegangen und habe so
nicht nur Dich gefunden, sondern nebenbei auch noch sehn können,
dass Dir die Mädchen wie am Schnürchen folgen. Besonders die Schwarze,
ein wahre Wild-Katze hat sich für Dich eingesetzt. Nun jeder nach
seinem Geschmack. Jedenfalls aber war es nicht nötig, dass Du den Um-
weg über den Nachbargarten gemacht hast, ich kenne den Weg."

Die Tür der Schule stand weit offen, man hatte sich nach der
Übersiedlung nicht einmal die Mühe genommen sie zuzuschieben,
die Verantwortung trug ja nach dem Abschied nur K. allein. Auch
war die Übersiedlung vollständig gewesen. Es war nichts zurückgeblie-
ben als die Michbach und der Rest Holz
schien zu fehlen, so als hätte man vorausgesehn dass er als er
satz die schließlich doch übernommene Verdienste mitbringen
werde.

Nun war's aber doch geschehn, was voraus zu sehen aber nicht zu ver-
hindern gewesen war. Frieda hatte ihn verlassen. Es mußte nichts end-
gültiges sein so schlimm war es nicht, Frieda war zurückzuerobern
sie war leicht von Fremden zu beeinflussen. gar von diesen Gehilfen,
welche Friedas Stellung für ähnlich der ihren hielten und nun
da sie gekündigt hatten auch Frieda dazu veranlasst hatten aber K.
mußte nur vor sie treten, an alles erinnern, was für ihn sprach
und sie war wieder (da seine reuevoll)

Above. The Villa Magdalene in Müritz on the Baltic Sea, where the Berlin Jewish People's Home had set up a resort in the summer of 1923. Kafka frequently visited this vacation colony when he was in Müritz with his sister Elli and her children in July of that year. It was here that he met Dora Diamant.

Left. Two photographs of Dora Diamant taken at this time.

Below. The beach and boat pier in Müritz.

Above. Two houses in Berlin where Kafka lived with Dora Diamant. *Left,* Grunewaldestrasse 13 in Berlin-Steglitz (November 1923 to January 1924). *Right,* Heidestrasse 25 in Berlin-Zehlendorf (February and March 1924), no longer standing.

Right. Corner of the Grunewaldestrasse and the town-hall square in Steglitz. During the winter months of inflation Kafka read the advance editions of the local daily paper posted in the display windows on the ground floor.

Below right. View of the Heidestrasse.
Below. The streetcar to the center of Berlin.

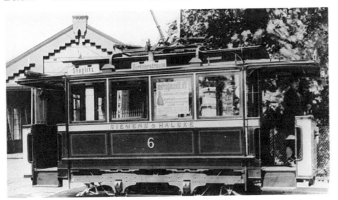

Above. Opening of the first printing of Kafka's final work, the short story "Josephine the Singer," in the 1924 Easter supplement to the *Prager Presse.* (See Appendix.)

Above left. Dr. Hoffmann's Sanatorium in Kierling, Lower Austria. Here, attended by Dora Diamant and Robert Klopstock, Kafka died on June 3, 1924.

Left. Views of the sanatorium.

Below. Kafka's death notice, in Czech and German. (See Appendix.)

The last photo-
graph, 1923 or
1924.

Above. Kafka's parents and Uncle Siegfried in Merano, 1926.

Above left. The parents at Bad Podiebrad, 1930.

Left. Kafka's grave in the Straschnitz Cemetery, Prague. Kafka's parents were buried in the same plot, the father in 1931, the mother in 1934.

Opposite. The first edition, with dust jacket, of *A Hunger Artist,* published in Berlin by the firm of "Die Schmiede" in 1924. Kafka lived long enough to correct proof for this final collection of stories; it was published soon after his death.

Franz Kafka

1901. At eighteen.

1905–1906. At twenty-two.

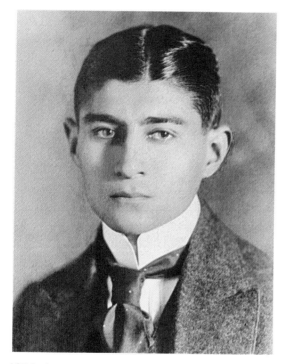

1910. At twenty-seven.

1915–1916. At thirty-two.

About 1917. At thirty-four.

About 1920. At thirty-six.

1921. At thirty-eight.

1923–1924. At forty.

German and Czech Versions of Place Names Used in This Book

Aussig: Ústí nad Labem
Dobrichowitz: Dobřichovice
Elbeteinitz: Týnec nad Labem
Franzensbad: Františkovy Lázně
Friedland: Frýdlant
Gablonz: Jablonec
Humpoletz: Humpolec
Iglau: Jihlava
Karlsbad: Karlovy Vary
Karlstein: Karlštejn
Kratzau: Chrastava
Kuchelbad: Chuchle
Kuttenberg: Kutná Hora
Leitmeritz: Litoměřice
Liboch: Liběchov
Libotz: Liboc
Maffersdorf: Vratislavice
Marienbad: Mariánské Lázně
Neustadt an der Tafelfichte: Nové Město po Smrk
Pilsen: Plzeň
Planá an der Luschnitz: Planá nad Lužnice
Podersam: Podhořany

Podiebrad: Poděbrady
Postelberg: Postoloorty
Prag (Prague): Praha
Raspenau: Raspenava
Reichenberg: Liberec
Roztok: Roztoky
Rumburg: Rumburk
Schelesen: Želízy
Schüttenhofen: Sušice
Spindelmühle: Spindleruv Mlýn
Spitzberg: Špičák
Stechowitz: Štěchovice
Strakonitz: Strakonice
Straschnitz: Strašnice
Tetschen: Děčin
Trautenau: Trutnov
Triesch: Třešt
Turnau: Turnov
Warnsdorf: Varnsdorf
Wossek: Osek
Zuckmantel: Zlate Hory
Zürau: Siřem

210

Appendix

The following translations of textual material within the illustrations (documents, letters, newspaper articles, passages from Kafka's manuscripts and published works) are, unless otherwise specified, by Arthur S. Wensinger. Full citations for the previously published translations can be found in the Partial List of Sources.

PAGE 97:

THE AEROPLANES IN BRESCIA, by Franz Kafka (Prague)

We have arrived. In front of the aerodrome itself there is another large area with suspicious-looking little wooden structures bearing signs quite different from what one would expect: Garage, Grand International Buffet, and so on. Monstrously fat beggars in small carts reach out and block our path. In our haste we are tempted simply to jump over them. We pass many people and many, in turn, pass us. We gaze up into the sky, the arena for today's activities. Thank God, nothing is flying yet! We do not bother to get out of the way, but no matter, no one runs us down. Italian cavalry soldiers are prancing about in the midst of a thousand carriages and wagons, coming toward them, pursuing them from behind. Order and catastrophe seem equally impossible.

PAGE 107:

CURRICULUM VITAE

I was born in Prague on July 3, 1883, attended the Altstädter Grammar School, then entered the Altstädter German *Gymnasium;* at eighteen I began my studies at the German Karl-Ferdinand University in Prague. After having passed the final state examinations, I became a junior law clerk in the office of Dr. Richard Löwy, Altstädter Ring. In June I passed the *rigorosum* in the history of law and was graduated with the degree of Doctor of Law.

By prearrangement with Dr. Löwy, I worked in the law office with the understanding that my purpose was to make the best use of my time, for from the beginning it was not my intention to remain there. I began this legal internship on October 1, 1906, and remained at the firm until October 1, 1907.

PAGE 108:

The Undersigned earnestly petitions the esteemed Board of Directors of the Workers Accident Insurance Company for the Kingdom of Bohemia for employment as junior assistant and supports this application with the following documentation:

The attached State Examination certificates (1–3) and the *absolutorium* (4) will furnish evidence that the applicant has successfully passed the three State Examinations at the Karl-Ferdinand University in Prague.

After having completed the three *rigorosa* at the same university on June 18, 1906, he earned the degree of Doctor of Law.

From April 1, 1906, to October 1, 1906, the applicant was employed as a junior law clerk (5), next undertook a judicial internship (6) until October 1, 1907, and since that date has been office clerk at the Assicurazioni Generali in Prague.

The applicant has both a written and oral command of German and Bohemian [i.e., Czech]; he is fluent in

French and, to a lesser extent, English. From February 3 until May 20 of the present year he was enrolled in the course for workmen's insurance at the Prague Commercial College and completed the examinations with the grades attested to on the attached certificate (7).

In 1906 the applicant was placed in category 3 and is thus exempt from military service.

Prague, June 20, 1908   Franz Kafka, Jur.D.

PAGE 114:

Not only all precautionary measures but all safety devices as well have failed in the face of this danger, either because they have proved to be totally insufficient, or because they have on the one hand lessened the danger (by securing the blade-slot with automatic blade-guards or by a diminution in the size of the blade-slot itself) but on the other hand actually increased it by not leaving enough space for the wood shavings to fall through, so that the blade-slot becomes clogged and the plane operator frequently incurs an injury to his fingers when he attempts to free the slot of the shavings.

PAGE 129:

But every day at least one line should be trained on me, as they now train telescopes on comets. And if then I should appear before that sentence once, lured by that sentence, just as, for instance, I was last Christmas, when I was so far gone that I was barely able to control myself and when I seemed really on the last rung of my ladder, which, however, rested quietly on the ground and against a wall. But what ground, what a wall! And yet that ladder did not fall, so strongly did my feet press it against the ground, so strongly did my feet raise it against the wall.

(Translation by Joseph Kresch)

PAGE 131:

EASTERN EUROPEAN JEWISH RECITATION EVENING

On Sunday the 18th [of February 1912] the recitation evening by the Warsaw actor Y. Löwy took place in the main auditorium of the Jewish Town Hall. After an excellent and charming opening address by Dr. Kafka, Herr Löwy commenced his offerings with several recitations and then gave us a great variety of both serious and humorous pieces, monologues, dramatic scenes, and songs. It was most interesting to hear these Eastern-Jewish poems and songs (some of them familiar to us in Prague) performed not only by an Eastern Jew but also without any touches of Western idiom. They consequently lost something of their artistic effectiveness, but, in return, gained a certain historical, documentary value. Before each section of the program, Herr Schneller energetically commented on its text with sensitive introductions. The audience, at first a little put off by the strangeness of the language, presently came round to the proper mood and a sympathetic understanding and repaid Herr Löwy's accomplishments with enthusiastic applause. The evening undoubtedly contributed much to a closer understanding of Eastern Jewish life and culture, and Herr Löwy, who acquitted himself as a powerful and persuasive performer, has good reason to be satisfied with the impression he made on his audience.

PAGE 141:

A GREAT COMMOTION

I sit in my room, at the very center of all the racket in the apartment. I can hear every door as it is slammed shut. The only noise I am spared is the footfalls of those passing through the doors as they slam. I can even hear the clank of the oven door being closed in the kitchen. My father breaks through the doors of my room and marches past with his dressing gown dragging behind him. Ashes are being scraped out of the stove in the

212

room next door. From the hallway Valli asks (and each word is a separate shout) whether Father's hat has been brushed yet. A hissing sound, a voice evidently suppressed out of kindness to me, only serves to exaggerate the shriek of the voice that replies. The latch on the apartment door snaps and the creaking hinges sound like a cough from an inflamed throat; the door opens further to the sound of a singing woman's voice and finally closes with a muffled, masculine thud, the most inconsiderate sound of all. Father has departed. And now begins the more gentle, more scatterbrained, the more dispiriting noise, ushered in by the voices of the two canary birds. It occurred to me earlier, and now with the canaries it occurs to me again, that perhaps I ought to open my door just a tiny crack, slither into the next room like a serpent, and groveling on the floor at the feet of my sisters and their Fräulein, beg them for quiet.

PAGE 142:

It was on a Sunday morning in the very height of spring. Georg Bendemann, a young merchant, was sitting in his own room on the second floor of one of a long row of gracefully built houses stretching beside the river, scarcely distinguishable from each other except in height and color. He had just finished a letter to an old friend of his who was now living abroad, had put ~~the letter~~ it into its envelope with a playful and deliberate gesture, and with his elbows propped on the desk was ~~looking gazing~~ looking out of the window at the river, the bridge, and the hills on the farther bank with their tender green. He was thinking about this friend, who had practically fled to Russia years before, being dissatisfied with his lack of success at home. Now he was carrying on a business in St. Petersburg which ~~was going~~ had flourished to begin with but which seemed for some time now to be in the doldrums, as the friend complained on his increasingly rare visits. ~~Georg on the other hand had remained at home.~~ So he was wearing himself out to no purpose in a foreign country, the outlandish full beard he wore failed to conceal the face Georg had known well since childhood, whose jaundiced coloration [indicated] a developing . . .

PAGE 143:

~~had been~~ to his parents' pride. With weakening grip he still held on, when he spied ~~through the~~ between the railings a motor-bus coming which would easily drown out the sound of his fall, called out in a low voice, "dear Parents, I have always loved you," and let himself fall. At this moment a nearly endless stream of traffic was going over the bridge.

56×17

392 $24 : 17 = 56 : x$

952 $24 = 3$

$"232$

23 This story, "The Judgment," I wrote at one sitting during the night of the 22nd–23rd, from ten o'clock at night to six o'clock in the morning. I was hardly able to pull my legs out from under the desk, they had got so stiff from sitting. The fearful strain and joy, how the story developed before me.

(Translation by Willa and Edwin Muir; changes by ASW)

PAGE 143 (BOTTOM):

Dear Supervisor!

I suffered a little fainting spell this morning and have a slight fever. For that reason I am staying at home. It is certainly not serious and I shall certainly be coming to the office today, but perhaps not until the afternoon.

PAGE 148:

II. What are we to do on these spring days that are now fast coming on? Early this morning the sky was gray, but if you go to the window now you will be taken unawares and lean your cheek against the latch of the casement. The sun is already setting, but down below you can still see it lighting up the face of the little girl who just strolls along, looking about, and at the same time you see her face eclipsed by the shadow of the man approaching from behind.

Then the man has already passed her by and the little girl's face is quite bright.

(Translation by Ernst Kaiser and Eithne Wilkins)

PAGE 152:

KURT WOLFF, PUBLISHERS / LEIPZIG / FORMERLY ERNST RO-WOHLT, PUBLISHERS / THE NEWEST DAY / NEW WRITING

Our intention is to bring together the most powerful examples of contemporary writing in a new publishing program, free from the restrictions imposed by literary journals. "The Newest Day" will be more than just another group of books, but less than a [formal] library. It is to be a series of creative works by our latest authors, produced out of the common experience of our time. Beginning immediately, we shall publish at intervals and at a low price (80 pfennigs for the paper-cover edition, 1½ marks for bound copies) the work of those writers whose character and quality are essential ingredients of this new spirit. As short but potent epitomes of their creators' ideas, these writings are intended to reach the widest possible readership at the lowest possible cost. "The Newest Day" recognizes no one clique, no one circle of friends or foes, no one city, and no one country. For this reason, and faithful to the promise implicit in its name, this program aims to bring together from the vital sources of our own day everything needed to assure it lasting value. *We ask the retail book trade to do its utmost in supporting our efforts to promote young, creative writers.*

Page 154:

As Gregor Samsa awoke one morning from uneasy dreams he found himself transformed in his bed into a gigantic insect. He was lying on his hard, as it were armor-plated, back and when he lifted his head a little he could see his dome-like brown belly divided into stiff arched segments on top of which the bed quilt could hardly keep in position and was about to slide off completely. His numerous legs, which were pitifully thin compared to the rest of his bulk, waved helplessly before his eyes.

What has happened to me? he thought. It was no dream. His room, a regular human bedroom, only rather too small, lay quiet between the four familiar walls. Above the table on which a collection of cloth samples was unpacked and spread out—Samsa was a commercial traveler—hung the picture which he had recently cut out of an illustrated magazine and put into a pretty gilt frame. It showed a lady, with a fur cap on and a fur stole, sitting upright and holding out to the spectator a huge fur muff into which the whole of her forearm had vanished!

Gregor's eyes turned next to the window, and the overcast sky—one could hear rain drops beating on the window gutter—made him quite melancholy. What about sleeping a little longer. . . .

(Translation by Willa and Edwin Muir)

Page 156:

STERNHEIM GIVES HIS FONTANE PRIZE TO A YOUNG WRITER FROM PRAGUE.

Carl Sternheim, whose play *The Candidate* will have its première at the Volksbühne Theater in Vienna this week, was awarded the Fontane Prize for his three stories, "Busekow," "Napoleon," and "Schulin," by Franz Blei, a member of this year's jury. The author accepted the honor associated with this prize and then passed the award money on to the young fiction writer from Prague Franz Kafka, in recognition of the latter's accomplishments as the author of the stories "Meditation," "The Stoker," and "The Metamorphosis."

"It's a remarkable piece of apparatus," said the officer to the explorer and surveyed with a certain air of admiration the apparatus which was after all quite familiar to him. The explorer seemed to have accepted merely out of politeness the Commandant's invitation to witness the execution of a soldier condemned to death for disobedience and insulting behavior to a superior. Nor did the colony itself betray much interest in this execution. At least, in the small sandy valley, a deep hollow surrounded on all sides by naked crags, there was no one present save the officer, the explorer, the condemned man, who was a stupid-looking wide-mouthed creature with bewildered hair and face, and the soldier. . . .

(Translation by Willa and Edwin Muir)

In spite of his ~~great~~ knowledge of men and the experience of the world which K. had acquired during his long service in the Bank, the company he met at dinner in the evenings had always impressed him as ~~something~~ particularly calculated to inspire respect, and he never denied in his inmost thoughts that it was a great honor for him to belong to such a society. It consisted almost exclusively of judges, ~~other court officials~~ prosecuting counsels, and lawyers, although a few ~~youngish~~ quite young officials and lawyers' clerks were also admitted; but they sat right at the bottom of the table and were only allowed to take part in the debates when questions were addressed to them directly, such questions being nearly always put in order to divert the rest of the company. Hasterer in particular, a prosecuting counsel who generally sat next to K., ~~loved~~ to [embarrass] ~~the gentleman~~ loved to [embarrass] the young men in this way.

(Translation by Willa and Edwin Muir; changes by ASW)

The horse was led forward. The man hesitated, the woman closed her eyes as a sign of agreement. A cavalry troop rode up from the highway. They all greeted one another.

The Vice-Secretary Dr. Franz Kafka is suffering from a medically confirmed catarrhal apicitis of the lung and has remained away from the office since September 11 of this year. Prague, 9/14 1917.

Resumed his duties at the office today. 5/2 1918

My dear Children! I wrote you on Sunday and hope that you have received my letter. Do write me how you are, especially whether you are healthy. Today I am sending you apples, pastries, and cocoa and hope that you will enjoy eating everything. I send you loving regards and remain your faithful Mother, Julie

It's a long time since I wrote to you, Frau Milena, and even today I'm writing only as the result of an incident. Actually, I don't have to apologize for my not writing, you know after all how I hate letters. All the misfortune of my life—I don't wish to complain, but to make a generally instructive remark—derives, one could say, from letters or from the possibility of writing letters. People have hardly ever deceived me, but letters always—and as a matter of fact not only those of other people, but my own. In my case this is a special misfortune of which I won't say more, but at the same time also a general one.

(Translation by Tania and James Stern)

[". . .] we came to an agreement. Everything's settled. I'm to be waiter in the Herrenhof, and Frieda is back in the taproom again. It's better for Frieda. There was no sense in her becoming your wife. And you haven't known how to value the sacrifice that she was prepared to make for you either. But the good soul had still some scruples left, perhaps she was doing you an injustice, she thought, perhaps you weren't with the Barnabas girl after all. Although of course there could be no doubt where you were, I went all the same so as to make sure of it once and for all; ~~but Frieda was sleeping poorly and was~~ for after all this worry Frieda deserved to sleep peacefully for once, not to mention myself. So I went and not only found you there, but was able to see incidentally as well that you had the girls on a string. The black one especially—a real wildcat—she's set her cap at you. Well, everyone to his taste. But all the same it wasn't necessary for you to take the round-about way through the next-door garden, I know that way."

The door of the school was standing wide open, after the move no one had even taken the trouble to close it. After the departure the responsibility was K.'s alone. In addition, the move had been complete, nothing had been left behind except the knapsack and a few articles of underwear, even the cane seemed to be missing, almost as if one could have anticipated that he would bring along in its place the unused willow switch.

So now the thing had come after all which he had been able to foresee, but not to prevent. Frieda had left him. It could not be final, it was not so bad as that, Frieda could be won back, it was easy for any stranger to influence her, even for those assistants, who considered Frieda's position much the same as their own and, now that they had given notice, had prompted Frieda to do the same, but K. would only have to show himself and remind her of all that spoke in his favor, and she would rue it and come back to him. . . .

(Translation by Willa and Edwin Muir; changes by ASW)

JOSEPHINE THE SINGER, by Franz Kafka

Our singer is called Josephine. Anyone who has not heard her does not know the power of song. There is no one but is carried away by her singing, a tribute all the greater as we are not in general a music-loving race. Tranquil peace is the music we love best; our life is hard, we are no longer able, even on occasions when we have tried to shake off the cares of daily life, to rise to anything so high and remote from our usual routine as music. But we do not much lament that; we do not get even so far; a certain practical cunning, which admittedly we stand greatly in need of, we hold to be our greatest distinction, and with a smile born of such cunning we are wont to console ourselves for all shortcomings, even supposing—only it does not happen—that we were to yearn once in a way for the kind of bliss which music may provide. Josephine is the sole exception; she has a love for music and knows too how to transmit it; she is the only one; when she dies, music—who knows for how long—will vanish from our lives.

(Translation by Willa and Edwin Muir; changes by ASW)

In deepest sorrow we announce that our son, Doctor of Law Franz Kafka, died on June 3, at the age of 41, in the Kierling Sanatorium near Vienna. The burial will take place on Wednesday afternoon, June 11, at 3:45, at the Jewish Cemetery in Straschnitz.

Prague, June 10, 1924. Hermann and Julie Kafka, the parents, in the name of the bereaved family.

We request that there be no visits of condolence.

Partial List of Sources

The longer passages quoted in the text, and several of those included in the Appendix, are from the following sources:

Page 11: Diary entry for December 25, 1911, *The Diaries of Franz Kafka, 1910–1913*, ed. Max Brod, trans. Joseph Kresch (New York: Schocken Books, 1948).

Page 13: Franz Kafka, *Letter to His Father* (written 1919), in *Dearest Father: Stories and Other Writings*, trans. Ernst Kaiser and Eithne Wilkins (New York: Schocken Books, 1954).

Page 13: Franz Kafka, "Fragments from Notebooks and Loose Pages," in *Dearest Father*.

Page 34: Kafka, *Letter to His Father*.

Page 35: Kafka to Oskar Pollak, January 27, 1904, Franz Kafka, *Letters to Friends, Family, and Editors*, trans. Richard and Clara Winston (New York: Schocken Books, 1977).

Page 35: Kafka, *Letter to His Father*.

Page 62: Quoted by Gustav Janouch, *Conversations with Kafka*, 2nd ed., rev. and enlarged, trans. Goronwy Rees (New York: New Directions, 1971).

Page 103: Kafka to Hedwig Weiler, October–November 1907, *Letters to Friends, Family, and Editors*.

Page 127: Diary entry for September 23, 1912, *Diaries of Franz Kafka, 1910–1913*.

Page 161: Diary entry for March 9, 1914, *The Diaries of Franz Kafka, 1914–1923*, ed. Max Brod, trans. Martin Greenberg with the cooperation of Hannah Arendt (New York: Schocken Books, 1949).

Page 161: Diary entry for August 15, 1914, ibid.

Page 162: Diary entry for January 24, 1915, ibid.

Page 162: Kafka to Felice Bauer, winter 1916–1917, quoted by Max Brod, *Franz Kafka: A Biography*, trans. G. Humphreys Roberts with Richard Winston (New York: Schocken Books, 1960).

Page 162: Franz Kafka, "Fifth Octavo Notebook," August 1917, in *Dearest Father*.

Page 185: Kafka to Milena Jesenská, April 1920, Franz Kafka, *Letters to Milena*, ed. Willy Haas, trans. Tania and James Stern (New York: Schocken Books, 1953).

Page 185: Kafka, *Letter to His Father*.

Page 186: Postcard from Kafka to Felix Weltsch, October 9, 1923, *Letters to Friends, Family, and Editors*.

Page 186: Kafka to Milena Jesenská, late autumn 1920, *Letters to Milena*.

Page 212: Diary entry, date not given, *Diaries of Franz Kafka, 1910–1913*.

Page 213: Franz Kafka, "The Judgment," *The Complete Stories*, ed. Nahum N. Glatzer, trans. Willa and Edwin Muir et al. (New York: Schocken Books, 1976).

Page 213: Franz Kafka, "Absent-minded Window-gazing," in *Dearest Father*.

Page 214: Franz Kafka, "The Metamorphosis," *The Complete Stories*.

Page 215: Franz Kafka, "In the Penal Colony," *The Complete Stories*.

Page 215: Franz Kafka, *The Trial*, trans. Willa and Edwin Muir, 4th ed. (New York: Schocken Books, 1968).

Page 215: Kafka to Milena Jesenská, 1922, *Letters to Milena*.

Page 216: Franz Kafka, *The Castle*, trans. Willa and Edwin Muir, 4th ed. (New York: Schocken Books, 1954).

Page 216: Franz Kafka, "Josephine the Singer," *The Complete Stories*.

Illustration Credits

Acknowledgments

In addition to those named in the foregoing list, I must acknowledge my gratitude to many other persons and institutions for their part in helping me to assemble this material over the past three decades:

Assicurazioni Generali, Bayerischer Hof, Ida Bergmann, Hugo Bergmann, Brigitte and Gottfried Bermann-Fischer, Jürgen Born, Max Brod, Roland Busch, Karel Černy, Pavel Eisner, Friedrich Feigl, Reinhold W. Feldmann, Rainer Groothuis, Frauke Grünwald, Willy Haas, H. von Hartungen, Karel Hiebel, Monika Hillen, Esther Hoffe, Václav Holý, Gustav Janouch, Jewish National and University Library, Jerusalem, Else Margarete Just, Constanze Knitter, Barbara König, Gabriele Kronenberg, Michael Krüger, Heinz Lunzer and the Dokumentationsstelle für Neuere Österreichische Literatur, Uta Martin, Malcolm Pasley, Friedrich Pfäfflin, Thomas Platt, Karel Projsa, Jaroslav Prokop, Puch-Werke, Graz, Wolfgang Ramsbott, David Rome, Věra Saudková, Pavel Scheufler, Salman Schocken, Erhard Senf, Vladimír Šlapeta, National Jewish Museum, National Archive, and City Archive in Prague, Marianne and Jirka Steiner, Technisches Museum für Industrie und Gewerbe, Vienna, Cordevole Volpi, Alfred Weber, Jiři Weil, Felix Weltsch, Daniel Westermann, Helen and Kurt Wolff, Gertrud Wührschmidt, Hanns "O." Zischler.

In particular, I would like to thank Barbara Herzbruch for her assistance—in discovering the path in Zuckmantel, for example—and for fending off the attack of the geese in Planá.

Alas, the beautiful motorcycle on page 51 unfortunately does not bear the model name of "Odradek" after all. It is no more than a good old Laurin & Klement. But it is the very model on which Kafka rode around Triesch and out into the countryside. And so, Odradek continues to answer our question about the origin of its name with the words "Address unknown." And laughs.

221

About the Author

Klaus Wagenbach, born in Berlin in 1930, worked as an editor before founding his own publishing house in 1964. He has concerned himself with Kafka since 1950, has written several classic studies about him, and has published editions of his works. Over the last thirty years, Wagenbach has collected the most complete Kafka archive in the world.